F-16

FIGHTING FALCON

F-16
FIGHTING FALCON

ROBBIE SHAW

Motorbooks International
Publishers & Wholesalers ®

ACKNOWLEDGEMENTS

My thanks to Peter Foster, Don Spering and Andy Thomson and General Dynamics Public Relations for their help in providing material for this publication, and the numerous USAF squadrons for their assistance. Unless otherwise credited all photographs were taken by the author using KODACHROME 64 film.

Robbie Shaw

AUTHOR'S NOTE

While this book was in the final stages of preparation the United States Air Force was in the process of a major reorganization, which entailed the change of designation of a number of units. For instance, Tactical Fighter Wings have become Fighter Wings, others, such as the 4th become simply Wing, depending on the composition of the unit. Therefore both old and new designations will be featured in captions, depending on the circumstances of the subject.

Front Cover. An F-16B of 323 Squadron, Royal Netherlands Air Force seen high over the North Sea near its Leeuwarden base.

This edition first published in 1996 by
Motorbooks International Publishers & Wholesalers,
729 Prospect Avenue, PO Box 1, Osceola, WI 54020 USA

© 1996 by Robbie Shaw

Library of Congress Cataloging-in-Publication Data Available.

ISBN 0-7603-0264-2

Printed and bound in Hong Kong

INTRODUCTION

Easily the best selling jet fighter in the free world today, the General Dynamics F-16 Fighting Falcon was conceived from a USAF requirement for a new small, lightweight, low-cost air superiority fighter. A total of five companies; Boeing, General Dynamics, Lockheed, LTV and Northrop put forward their proposals for the Lightweight Fighter (LWF) program. Eventually three of these proposals were discarded, and on the 13 April 1972 a contract for the construction of two General Dynamics YF-16s and two Northrop YF-17s was issued. These two types were selected to participate in a year-long Air Force evaluation programme, with the prospect of a multi-billion dollar order for the successful candidate. The evaluation programme was under the direction of the USAF Aeronautical Systems Division at Wright-Patterson AFB (Air Force Base), Ohio, with each aircraft undertaking over 400 hours of test flying, primarily at Edwards AFB, California, home of the Air Force Flight Test Center. General Dynamics designed the aircraft with advanced aerodynamics and structural strength very much in mind, but at the same time employing advanced composite materials, including reinforced plastics. This strong, but relatively light airframe, combined with a powerful F100 engine gave the aircraft a high thrust/weight ratio, enabling the type to perform with exceptional manoeuvrability and acceleration.

The prototype YF-16 was rolled out at Forth Worth on 13 December 1973, and was then transported by C-5 Galaxy to Edwards AFB for its maiden flight which occurred on 20 January 1974. This first flight however was totally unplanned. During a high-speed taxi test the pilot encountered some oscillations and decided the best escape was to quickly become airborne. A few minutes and one circuit later the aircraft was landed safely, and the official maiden flight took place two weeks later on 2 February. The second YF-16 was delivered a few weeks later. Over the next eleven months both the YF-16 and YF-17 were put through exhaustive tests at Edwards, and during these evaluations they were pitted against a number of different aircraft types. During this time the YF-16 achieved speeds in excess of Mach 2 and flew at heights over 60,000ft (18,300m). Manoeuvres up to 9G were executed, and a large number of weapons in the inventory expended during these very successful trials where the aircraft either met, or exceeded all expectations.

The single-engined lightweight YF-16 was in contrast to the previous generation of US-built twin-engined heavyweights such as the F-4 and F-111, and the new F-15 Eagle. In that year-long evaluation programme the YF-16 flew against these and many other types, including a captured MiG-21. The YF-16 proved that, not only could it out-perform any current fighter in aerial combat, but that its low fuel consumption meant that it could remain on station twice as long as some other aircraft, such as the F-4 Phantom. In September 1974 the Department of Defense announced that the winner of the evaluation programme, now retitled Air Combat Fighter (ACF), would be announced in January 1975. On the 13th of that month the Secretary of State for Defense announced that the F-16 had been selected, and full-scale engineering development authorised. The original air superiority role had also been expanded to include an air-to-surface role, including the provision for all-weather radar. Attempts to induce the US Navy also to select the type failed, and they ultimately selected the F-18 Hornet, itself derived from the unsuccessful YF-17; the safety aspect of a twin-engined fighter for carrier operations no doubt being a significant factor.

Whilst the evaluation programme was under way, watching in the wings in anticipation were the European NATO allies Belgium, Denmark, the Netherlands and Norway. All four were anxiously seeking a replacement for their ageing F-104 Star-fighters, in what was dubbed the Sale of the Century. No doubt influenced by the USAF decision, the F-16 was the type selected in preference to the Saab Viggen and Dassault Mirage F1, which produced the predictable howls of protest from the French. Production lines were set up in both Belgium and the Netherlands to produce aircraft for the four countries. At Gosselies, SABCA produced aircraft for the Belgian and Danish Air Forces, with initial orders for 102 and forty-eight aircraft respectively, whilst at Fokker's Schiphol factory eighty-four and seventy-two were the initial orders for the Dutch and Norwegian Air Forces. Co-production contracts worth billions of dollars have been placed with the European manufacturers by General Dynamics and Pratt & Whitney. This amounted to ten per cent of the procurement value of the first 650 aircraft for the USAF, forty per cent for the aircraft acquired by their own air forces, and fifteen per cent procurement value of export sales.

Once the type had been selected the USAF quickly decided to equip the F-16 with a more powerful multi-mode look-down radar, which required a slightly larger nose-cone. The first batch of eight aircraft were pre-production machines for use in the development programme, and the USAF indicated it planned to acquire 1,388 F-16s. These pre-production aircraft differed in a number of respects from the YF-16s, including an increase in structural strength by twenty-five per cent to compensate for the high G manoeuvres. The fuselage was increased by 13.7in (0.35m), but because of a shorter nose-cone the actual length is 3.1in (0.08m) less. The wing area was increased by 20sq ft (1.86m) and the horizontal tails by fifteen per cent. The two-seat F-16B model has the same dimensions, but internal fuel capacity is reduced by seventeen per cent to make way for the second cockpit.

The first production F-16A made its maiden flight on the 7 August 1979. Although designed primarily as an air superiority fighter, during the evaluation programme the F-16 proved it had the makings of an excellent air-to-ground warplane and, contrary to expectations, it was in this role that the USAF employed the F-16A which entered operational service with the 388th Tactical Fighter Wing (TFW) at Hill AFB, Utah in January 1979. The Wing was declared 'combat ready' in October 1980, and in March the following year Hill's 4th Tactical Fighter Squadron deployed twelve aircraft to Flesland in Norway under 'Coronet Falcon', the first overseas deployment of the F-16. Coincidental with the 388th TFW receiving its aircraft, the Belgian Air Force received its first machines from the SABCA production line at Gosselies, equipping No 1 Wing at Beauvechain in the air defence role. One month later the first Dutch aircraft were delivered to Leeuwarden, and in January 1980 Denmark and Norway received their first aircraft. That month also saw the first export deliveries from Fort Worth with the first batch of two-seat F-16Bs for Israel, although had it not been for the revolution against the Shah, Iran would have been the first export customer with an initial order for 160 aircraft. The initial Israeli order was for seventy-five F-16A/Bs under the 'Peace Marble' programme, and subsequently a large number of F-16C/Ds have been acquired. Meanwhile at McDill AFB, Florida, the 56th Tactical Fighter Training Wing (TFTW) was transitioning from the F-4E Phantom to the F-16 Fighting Falcon, the name officially assigned to the aircraft by the USAF on 21 July 1980. The 474th TFW at Nellis quickly followed suit. The 388th TFW continued to set the pace, and in June 1981 deployed aircraft to the Royal Air Force tactical bombing competition at

Lossiemouth where the F-16s swept the board, beating USAFE F-111s and RAF Buccaneers and Jaguars.

The first USAF unit overseas to equip with the Falcon was the famous 8th TFW 'Wolf Pack' at Kunsan, Republic of Korea in September 1981. Here the 35th and 80th Tactical Fighter Squadrons (TFS) traded in their tired F-4D Phantoms in favour of the new 'electric jet', as the type was often nicknamed. A few months later United States Air Forces Europe received the first of the influx with the 50th TFW at Hahn being the recipient. They were quickly followed by the 401st TFW at Torrejon Air Base on the outskirts of Madrid, whilst back in the US deliveries of the F-16 continued to the 31st TFW at Homestead AFB, Florida, and the 58th TFTW at Luke AFB, Arizona.

The manoeuvrability and high thrust/weight ratio makes the F-16 an ideal aircraft for aerial demonstrations, so it was no surprise when, in 1982, it was announced that the USAF's Aerial Demonstration Squadron the 'Thunderbirds' would equip with the type, replacing T-38 Talon trainers. It was 1985 however before the team received its aircraft with modified Pratt & Whitney F-100-PW-220 engines.

In Tactical Air Command (TAC) the ageing but efficient Phantom was rapidly being displaced by the F-16, the 347th TFW at Moody AFB, Georgia was followed by the 363rd TRW at Shaw AFB, South Carolina which was re-designated a Tactical Fighter Wing when it disposed of its RF-4C recce' Phantoms. Further overseas units included the newly-formed 432nd TFW at Misawa, Japan, and the 86th TFW at Ramstein in the Federal Republic of Germany.

Over the next few years deliveries continued to the NATO countries and the USAF, and in 1983 the first Air National Guard (ANG) unit, South Carolina's 157th TFS, exchanged its A-7Ds for the F-16. The following year the Air Force Reserve's (AFRES) first recipient of the type converted. This was the 466th TFS at Hill AFB, the last unit to fly the ageing F-105 Thunderchief. Since then numerous Guard and some more Air Force Reserve Squadrons have converted to the F-16, whilst export sales thrived. Following the peace accord with Israel, the US Congress approved the sale of the type to Egypt. The first of a batch of forty F-16A/Bs were delivered in March 1982 under the 'Peace Vector' programme, and the Egyptians have since received further batches of the more capable C and D models. The first Asian customer was Pakistan who placed an order for forty F-16A/Bs in 1981, and the first of these were delivered late the following year. At the same time, the Pakistan Air Force required these aircraft to deter Soviet aircraft transgressing its border from neighbouring Afghanistan, replacing ageing Shenyang F-6s. A further two batches totalling seventy-one aircraft were ordered, however, because of political differences with the US over the issue of Pakistan's nuclear policy these were never delivered due to an arms embargo, and some are currently stored at Davis-Monthan AFB, Arizona. In 1983 Venezuela became the first, and so far only South American nation to take the F-16 into its inventory with the acquisition of eighteen A and six B models. Further export customers for the more basic A/B models include Thailand, who received eighteen in 1988, and has since placed an order for a further batch of sixteen. Singapore placed an order for a modest batch of eight aircraft which were delivered in 1988, though these aircraft remained in the US for crew training, and did not arrive in Singapore until January 1990. Following the news that the tiny island nation of Singapore was to acquire the F-16 and take its force of offensive aircraft to over 100, its near neighbour Indonesia, barely a spitting distance across the narrow Straits of Malacca, decided to order F-16s to boost its modest air defence assets. Deliveries of the twelve aircraft order were completed during 1990.

A major improvement in capability resulted with the introduction of the F-16C, which has a Hughes APG-68 multi-mode radar, giving better range and resolution than the Westinghouse APG-66

fitted to the A and B models. Other improvements include more advanced avionics and the capability to carry newer weapons, such as AGM-65D Maverick, AGM-88A HARM and AIM-120 AMRAAM depending on the batch of C model aircraft. The C model can be distinguished by the fillet at the leading edge of the base of the vertical fin, which has a blade antenna protruding from it. This was intended to house an airborne self-protection jammer as used by US Navy fighter aircraft, however due to financial restrictions this programme was abandoned. A number of C model aircraft are powered by the General Electric F110 engine which provides about 5,000lb (2,268kg) more thrust than Pratt & Whitney's F100. Aircraft fitted with the F110 have a larger engine intake. The two-seat variant of the C is the F-16D, and later production C/D models can carry the LANTIRN (Low Altitude Navigation and Targetting Infra-Red for Night) pod. Produced by the Martin-Marietta company, the system comprises two pods, one for navigation using terrain-following radar and FLIR (Forward Looking Infra-Red), and the other is the targetting pod. The latter allows automatic target acquisition and stand-off target identification by day and night, automatic target stand-off for multiple launch of Maverick missiles, autonomous laser-guided bomb delivery and precision air-to-ground laser ranging. When using this system the navigation pod is carried on the port side, and the targetting pod on the starboard side underneath the jet intake. To accommodate these pods the undercarriage doors have a bulge in them, and the landing gear itself has been beefed up to take the extra weight.

Early exports of the C/D variants were to established operators of the A/B models; Egypt and Israel, though the first deliveries were to a new customer, the Republic of Korea Air Force (RoKAF). The RoKAF ordered a batch of thirty-two aircraft in December 1981, and under programme 'Victory Falcon' the first of these was delivered in March 1986. A further four aircraft were ordered in 1988 to make up for attrition. The F-16 was also a leading contender in the Korea Fighter Program, where a total of 120 aircraft would be acquired, but lost out to the F-18 in what proved to be a controversial decision. In an amazing turnaround however the F-18 deal was cancelled, and an agreement to acquire further F-16s signed instead. The plans for these 120 aircraft call for Korean involvement in the production of the aircraft. The first twelve will be built and flown in the US, the next thirty-six will be assembled in Korea from US-made parts, and the final seventy-two will be totally built in Korea. One of the most important orders was that by Turkey in September 1983, when it was announced that 160 aircraft were to be acquired, comprising 132 F-16Cs and twenty-eight F-16Ds to replace ageing F-104 Starfighters. More importantly, the programme included setting up a new company, TUSAS Aerospace Industries (TAI), and building a production factory at Murted Air Base near Ankara. Quite an achievement for a country which had no aviation industry! The first eight aircraft were built by General Dynamics at Fort Worth, and the remaining 152 by TUSAS. The first Turkish-built aircraft made its maiden flight on 20 October 1987, having been rolled out of a production hangar where only three and a half years earlier there was barren land. Delivery of that aircraft was two months ahead of schedule, and a further forty aircraft have since been ordered. General Dynamics have been delighted with the quality of work produced by TUSAS. The company builds the aircraft from the rear of the cockpit with materials imported from the US, as the quality of aluminium used is not available in Turkey. Once the Texas-made cockpit section is married to the TUSAS-made aircraft, the engines, which are also manufactured in Turkey are fitted to the aircraft. After systems' checks and engine runs are completed the aircraft is test flown by TUSAS pilots, usually two to three flights are undertaken before the aircraft is flown by a US pilot for final acceptance. Once this has happened the aircraft is accepted by General Dynamics, who hand the aircraft over to the USAF who in turn hand it to the Turkish Air Force. Although this sounds a rather long-winded procedure, legally it has to be done this way as the contract is between the US and Turkish governments, with the USAF acting on their behalf. Such is the success of the TUSAS product that the company will soon produce aircraft for the latest batch ordered by the Egyptian Air Force. It has also been contracted by General Dynamics to produce centre fuselage, wings and tail sections for USAF aircraft, and the first batch of these have already been shipped to the Fort Worth production line, an excellent endorsement of the quality of the TUSAS product. After Turkey the next export customer for the Fighting Falcon was Turkey's NATO ally, but historic enemy, Greece. Forty F-16C/Ds were ordered in January 1987, and the first aircraft was handed over in November the following year. The latest customer to have received the F-16 is the Bahrain Amiri Air Force which received its eight C and four D models under project 'Peace Crown' in 1990, and these aircraft were used in action against Iraqi forces in the Gulf War.

Over the past few years many Air National Guard air defence units have converted from the F-4 and F-106 to the F-16A, these aircraft being handed down from Tactical Air Command units re-equipping with the F-16C. Some modifications were carried out on these aircraft, including provision to carry the AIM-7 Sparrow and AIM-120 AMRAAM missiles, and fitting high frequency radios and a searchlight for visual identification of targets during night intercepts. Some 270 F-16A/Bs were due to receive these modifications to ADF (Air Defense Fighter) standard, and these aircraft can be identified by the searchlight on the port side of the nose and by the avionics bulge at the base of the fin.

In January 1985 the US Navy announced the selection of the F-16 for use in the aggressor training role, supplementing A-4 Sky-hawks and F-5E Tigers. These aircraft have the designation F-16N, and the first of twenty-six aircraft, including four two-seat TF-16Ns were delivered to Naval Fighter Squadron VF-126 in April 1987. A further three Naval units have since received the type.

One role that I'm sure the manufacturer never envisaged for the F-16 is that of Close Air Support (CAS), the speciality of the A-10 Thunderbolt. However, a former A-10 unit, the New York Air National Guard's 138th TFS currently operates a batch of early build F-16As in this role using the GPU-5A Pave Claw 30mm cannon pod. It is quite conceivable that further batches, including F-16Cs will be made available for this role. Both the A-10 and the 138th TFS F-16s performed with distinction during the Gulf War. This conflict however was not the Fighting Falcon's combat début, that honour fell to the Israeli DF in June 1981 with the well-known raid on the Iraqi nuclear reactor at Osirak. Subsequently, Israeli F-16s have on a number of occasions tangled with Syrian MiGs, the result being an enviable, and almost unbelievable kill ratio in favour of the General Dynamics product. Subsequently Fighting Falcons played a major part in the air offensive during operation Desert Storm in the war against Iraq, whilst Pakistani F-16s have

Part of an F-16 line-up at the London (Ontario) International Air Show 1990, where the main event was a gathering of Fighting Falcons. Aircraft from many different USAF units attended the event, though for geographical reasons no European-based aircraft were present. The first three aircraft display the markings of squadrons from the Michigan, Arizona and Kansas Air National Guard.

been involved in several skirmishes and claimed a number of kills against Afghan aircraft that have strayed into Pakistani airspace. The Pakistan Air Force have also lost an F-16 in one such skirmish, though the reason for the loss has never been confirmed.

Over the years some of the pre-production aircraft have received intensive modifications for research purposes, such as the YF-16/CCV. This aircraft (72-1567) was rebuilt in late 1975 and became the USAF's Flight Dynamics Laboratory Control Configured Vehicle (CCV), testing advanced fly-by-wire technology. These tests were completed in July 1977. Another machine, (75-0750) became the F-16/AFTI (Advanced Fighter Technology Integration) aircraft, and was first flown in this configuration on 10 July 1982. It was fitted with a digital flight control system and fuselage mounted ventral foreplanes, permitting decoupled or six degrees of freedom flight modes, and also providing integrated manoeuvrability capability for making flat turns without sideslip. Later this aircraft was involved in the AMAS (Automated Manoeuvre and Attack System) programme, and then became the AFTI/CAS aircraft for extensive communications trials with ground troops with regard to target information and acquisition. Probably the most interesting and promising development was the F-16XL. The XL may have stood for extra large, as the two aircraft in this configuration featured a new composite-skinned cranked arrow-shaped enlarged wing, double the area of that on the standard F-16. The fuselage was lengthened by 4ft 8in (1.42m) which meant the amount of fuel carried internally was increased by an amazing eighty-five per cent. The shape of the wing allowed tandem semi-conformal weapons carriage. Bomb ejectors were mounted directly to the wing structure to take advantage of the more stable underwing flow. The F-16XL had seventeen stores stations on twenty-nine hardpoints under the wing and fuselage, enabling it to carry double the weapon load of a standard F-16A from a runway only two-thirds the length. The better cruise efficiency, increased internal fuel capacity and lower weapon carriage drag resulted in a forty-eight per cent increase in combat radius on internal fuel, and an eighty-seven per cent increase with external drop-tanks over the F-16A model. The F-16XL was in competition with the McDonnell-Douglas F-15E Strike Eagle for a USAF order as a dual role air defence/ground attack fighter, and during this evaluation was known as the F-16E. Unfortunately for General Dynamics the F-15E won the evaluation, and although the USAF allocated funds for continuing development of the XL, to be known as the F-16F, this was eventually terminated in November 1985. These F-16XLs are however still an important asset, and are currently in use with NASA's Dryden Flight Research Facility on laminar flow research work.

Another F-16 development which fell by the wayside was the F-16/79. This was a lower cost F-16 powered by the older but well-established J79 engine and aimed at the export market. F-16B 75-0752 was fitted with the J79 powerplant and first flew in this configuration on 29 October 1980: however the type failed to win any orders and the project was abandoned. As yet no dedicated reconnaissance version of the F-16 is available off the shelf, though development trials have been undertaken using an ATARS (Advanced Tactical Air Reconnaissance System) pod on the centre-line pylon. The pod houses a variety of sensors, including a video tape system that allows images to be transmitted via data-link to a ground station, providing real-time intelligence. The USAF has shown interest in, and needs such a system to replace the few remaining Air National Guard RF-4C Phantom units, however to date no orders have been forthcoming.

One area where an F-16 development has met with success is the selection by Japan to meet its FS-X requirement for an anti-shipping aircraft to replace its fleet of Mitsubishi F-1s. The type will be jointly developed by both the US and Japan, subject to agreement over technology transfer, which the two countries are currently in dispute. It will feature an enlarged wing and lengthened fuselage with greater internal fuel capacity. It is also planned to be fitted with canards and have a comprehensive suite of mission avionics, including a phased-array radar. In Japan the prime contractor is Mitsubishi Heavy Industries, though US companies will retain forty per cent of the work-share as well as access and share rights to any new-derived technology. The aft fuselage will be made in the US, and the aircraft will be powered by the General Electric F110-GE-129 engine. The Japanese require 130 of these aircraft, and possibly as many as 170. The prototype is due to fly in late 1995, and for the type to be in squadron service by the end of the decade. No decision has yet been made as to how many of these aircraft will be two-seaters, but such a development may be a timely replacement for the Japanese Air Self Defence Force (JASDF) fleet of T-2 advanced trainers.

The F-16 has certainly proved itself an extremely efficient and potent warplane, and the four European NATO allies who purchased the type have subsequently ordered additional aircraft, with Portugal soon to join the club and receive seventeen F-16As and three F-16Bs. The list of export customers will certainly expand. The Republic of China Air Force (RoCAF) has been offered 150 F-16s by the US Government, however these are A/B models and not the more potent C/D models which the RoCAF requires. It may well be that the Taiwanese will say thanks, but no thanks, and go for further Mirage 2000s instead. At the time of writing, over 3,000 F-16s have been delivered, and I have no doubt that the aircraft will become the best selling jet fighter of its era.

As this book was in the final stages of completion it transpires that there is no longer such an aircraft as the General Dynamics F-16, as that company's aircraft production facilities have been bought by the Lockheed Aircraft Corporation. Lockheed F-16 Fighting Falcon – no, it just doesn't sound right!

(Right)
An F-16C takes-off from a gloomy Farnborough to commence its display at the 1988 show.

TEST AND DEVELOPMENT

The prototype YF-16A visited Europe in the summer of 1975, the highlight of the visit was the appearance at the Paris Air Show. Other venues included Alconbury, where the aircraft appeared at the annual air show. This particular aircraft has since been retired and is now preserved at the Hampton Museum, located just outside the main gate of Langley AFB, Virginia.

The Air Force Flight Test Center at Edwards AFB, California has a variety of aircraft on strength for test purposes, which are operated by the 416th Test Squadron (TS), 412th Test Wing (TW) (formerly the 6512th TS, 6510th TW). A large number of F-16 Fighting Falcons and T-38 Talons are employed, the latter being extensively used on chase-plane duties. Additional F-16Bs have recently been acquired and have replaced F-4 Phantoms which have now been retired. F-16A 79-408 carries Air Force Flight Test Center's 'ED' tailcode and Air Force Systems Command insignia on the fin. Since this photograph was taken Air Force Systems Command has ceased to exist, and has been absorbed into Air Materiel Command.

(Above)
Another component of Air Force Systems Command was the Munitions Systems Division at Eglin AFB, Florida, which is allocated the appropriate tailcode 'ET' – Eglin Test. As its title suggests the Division is responsible for the development and testing of airborne weapons, a task which is delegated to the 3247th TS, 3246th TW, which operates the F-4, F-15, F-16 and F-111. This unit has since been redesignated the 40th TS, 46th TW under the Air Force Development Test Center, Air Materiel Command. Illustrated is F-16A 82-985 'ET' climbing steeply with vortices trailing from the leading edge over the wing.

(Left)
On a beautiful Canadian summer's day, 82-985 'ET' taxies to its parking spot at the London (Ontario) International Air Show. Although built as an F-16A, the aircraft now has the tail of an F-16C with the extended forward fillet and two additional aerials.

11

Also Eglin-based, but a component of Air Combat Command, is the Tactical Air Warfare Center's 4485th TS which operates a small number of F-4s and F-16s. One of the latter, F-16A 79-328 is illustrated wearing the unit's 'OT' (Operational Test) tailcode. Under the reorganisation programme the unit is now the 85th TS, 79th TEG, and operates A, C and D models of the Fighting Falcon.

UNITED STATES AIR FORCE
AIR COMBAT COMMAND (ACC)

As this book was being prepared the effects of Glasnost and the ending of the Cold War has seen almost unprecedented changes in the USAF structure. The build-up of the Reagan era no longer exists, instead a number of units and bases have already closed down or are in the process of doing so. A further round of savage defence cuts is also extremely likely in the near future, and a number of famous Wings and bases seem likely to disappear into the history books. A major reorganisation of the command structure has seen Tactical Air Command (TAC) renamed Air Combat Command (ACC), and the first integrated Wing is now in existence at Seymour-Johnson AFB, which operates F-15Es and KC-10s in the same Wing. This reorganisation has gone a step further with the establishment of integrated Wings operating a variety of types, such as offensive and defensive fighters, as well as tanker and support aircraft. One such Wing is the 366th Wing at Mountain Home AFB, Idaho. The unit currently comprises six squadrons and six different types ; B-52G, KC-135R, F-15C, F-15E, F-16C and EF-111A. All carry the Wing's 'MO' tailcode, though for logistical and operational reasons the B-52s are based at Castle AFB, California. A further change has seen Tactical Fighter Squadrons and Wings (TFS & TFW) now become simply Fighter Squadrons and Wings (FS & FW). Air Combat Command has recently transferred the F-15E and F-16 training unit, the 58th FW at Luke AFB to the recently formed Air Education and Training Command. This now leaves only five F-16s Wings on strength, and one of these, the 56th FW at McDill is to disband in 1994 and its training role to be absorbed by the 58th FW at Luke AFB, Arizona. The remaining Wings are ; the 347th at Moody, 363rd at Shaw, 388th at Hill and the 31st at Homestead. The latter unit is in a state of limbo as Homestead AFB, Florida, was virtually destroyed by Hurricane Andrew in 1992, and its three squadrons have been dispersed to Moody and Shaw and integrated into the Wings at those bases until a decision has been taken as to the future of Homestead. The Command has also recently activated a new squadron, the 74th which is a component of the 23rd Wing at Pope AFB, North Carolina. First deliveries to this new unit took place in March 1993.

(Below)
Air Combat Command's Air Demonstration Squadron better known as the 'Thunderbirds' are based at Nellis AFB, Nevada and operate a team of six F-16Cs, though the team previously flew the A model until 1992. The team travels extensively throughout North America, and every few years undertakes a tour to another continent. Four of the team's aircraft were caught by the camera during a manoeuvre at Osan AB, Republic of Korea during a 1987 tour of the Far East.

(Above)
Thunderbird No 4 (81-667) taxies back to the ramp at Edwards AFB after a display at the sprawling desert base. The team received its F-16s in March 1985, having previously operated the Northrop T-38 Talon. I have witnessed Thunderbirds' displays on three occasions and, in comparison to the top European display teams I have always found their performances somewhat disappointing and rather staid. The marathon hype which preceeds each display certainly does not help. This is not meant to be a reflection on the pilots, but is due to the rules enforced on the team by higher authority which does not allow the team to display the F-16 to anything like its capability.

(Right)
Also located at Nellis, but for an altogether different purpose, is the Tactical Fighter Weapons Center. The Center is responsible for the development of combat tactics within the USAF and has two evaluation squadrons and an aggressor squadron within the 57th Fighter Weapons Wing (FWW). The majority of the Wing's aircraft wear the unit's black and yellow checks on the top of the fin, as on F-16B 79-422 'WA' of the 422nd TES. Since this photograph was taken the USAF reorganisation has seen the 57th FWW become the 57th FW with two component squadrons; the 414th Composite Training Squadron and the 422nd Test and Evaluation Squadron. (GB Aircraft Slides)

F-16A 80-539 'WA' of the 57th Fighter Weapons Wing was photographed at CFB Cold Lake, Alberta where it was participating in a Maple Flag exercise.

(Right)
The first operational Wing to equip with the F-16 was the 388th at Hill AFB, Utah in January 1980, and the Wing's 4th Tactical Fighter Squadron became operational later that year. Within six months the squadron undertook its first overseas deployment with the F-16 when twelve aircraft were deployed to Flesland, Norway. F-16A 78-046 'HL' was photographed from a KC-135 tanker returning from the Norwegian deployment.

(Below)
The 57th used to be comprised of two aggressor squadrons, the 64th and 65th, both equipped with the F-5E Tiger II. By the time these words are read the 65th will have disbanded, leaving the 64th to operate a small number of F-16Cs. These aircraft participate in Red Flag exercises and travel around the US to other fighter bases teaching combat tactics. A small number have also acquired a desert style camouflage pattern as seen on this F-16C on approach to Nellis. Since this photograph was taken the 64th has been retitled the 414 CTS (Composite Training Squadron).
(Peter Foster)

(Above)
When the 388th received its first F-16s, the 16th TFTS (Tactical Fighter Training Squadron) undertook the training role and as such the bulk of its aircraft were two-seat F-16Bs. The unit was the first operational F-16 squadron and adopted blue and white checks to identify their aircraft, as seen on this line-up headed by F-16B 78-084 'HL'.

(Left)
After a short while the 16th became an operational squadron and transferred its training role to the 56th TFTW at McDill AFB, Florida. The squadron was rather short-lived as an F-16 unit, and was the first to give up the type when it disbanded in June 1986, its aircraft being transferred to the Montana Air National Guard. Photographed at Hill in 1981 is F-16B 78-086 'HL'.

(Above)
Another component of the 388th TFW is the 34th TFS which is nicknamed 'Rams'. Sharing the ramp at CFB (Canadian Forces Base) Cold Lake with aircraft from the 347th TFW is F-16A 82-972 'HL'. Note the squadron nickname within the red fin band. The unit has since transitioned to the F-16C and changed designation under the restructuring programme.

(Right)
The final squadron of the 388th TFW is the 421st TFS 'Black Widows' which has also recently transitioned to the F-16C. This photograph of F-16A 79-303 'HL' was taken soon after the squadron received its first 'electric jet' in late 1981. The 388th is now known as a Fighter Wing and comprises three squadrons; the 4th, 34th and 421st.

The next Wing to equip was the 56th Tactical Training Wing at McDill AFB, Florida. Formerly an F-4 training unit the Wing comprised initially three training squadrons; 61st, 62nd and 63rd, to be joined later by the 72nd. The Wing had a mix of both F-16As and Bs, though has since upgraded to the C and D models. Taxying out for a training mission is F-16B 80-626 'MC' of the 61st TFTS. The 56th has been redesignated a Fighter Wing, however the 61st Fighter Squadron and the Wing was deactivated in 1994 and the training role absorbed by the 58th FW at Luke AFB, Arizona.

(Above)
F-16A 78-050 'MC' is towed to the flight-line after maintenance. The blue fin band identifies it as belonging to the 62nd TFTS, 56th TTW. This squadron was deactivated with the Wing in 1994.

(Right)
Although in a training unit, instructor pilots need to maintain currency in weapons' delivery and tactics, and take every opportunity to participate in exercises like Maple Flag at CFB Cold Lake where F-16A 80-496 'MC' was photographed. This 63rd TFTS machine is carrying practice bombs for a mission on the nearby ranges. Now redesignated a Fighter Squadron, the 63rd has since transferred to the 58 FW at Luke, the USAF's primary F-16 training unit.

All four squadrons at McDill traded their F-16A and B models for newer upgraded Cs and Ds. The 63rd now carry the squadron nickname 'Panthers' within their red fin band as shown on F-16C 87-344 'MC'.

In common with many F-16 units the 309th TFS now carries the unit name 'Wild Ducks' within the squadron colour at the top of the fin, as seen on F-16A 82-944 'HS'. Due to the devastation at Homestead caused by Hurricane Andrew the 309th FS is currently operating under the 363rd FW at Shaw, whilst sister squadrons 307th and 308th 'Knights' are at Moody with the 347th FW.

The other major F-16 training unit is the 58th Fighter Wing at Luke AFB, Arizona which is home to four F-16 training squadrons of the Air Education and Training Command (AE&TC). It was previously known as a Tactical Fighter Training Wing and was co-located with the 405th Tactical Training Wing with four F-15 training squadrons. The 405th has since disbanded and F-15E training is now undertaken by the 58th. When the 58th transitioned from F-4D Phantoms to the F-16s in 1983 it also changed the tailcode from 'LA' to 'LF', standing for Luke Falcons. With the undercarriage doors still retracting, F-16C 88-464 'LF' takes-off from London (Ontario) to give a solo display at the annual airshow.

The four training squadrons of the 58th TTW were the 310, 311, 312 and 314th. The 314th was the most recently formed (October 1986) and received F-16Cs, whilst the other three units converted from the A and B models to the C and D. Illustrated is F-16C 88-464 'LF' of the 311th TFTS 'Sidewinders'.

(Left)
Against a background of crystal clear blue skies 312th TFTS 'Scorpions' F-16D 83-174 'LF' makes an approach to Luke AFB. This aircraft was the first production F-16D. The 312th was responsible for training many aircrew from export customers, one of the most recent being those from the Singapore Defence Force. The squadron has however now disbanded and this role assumed by other units within the Wing, which has recently been expanded by the transfer of the 63rd Fighter Squadron from McDill. (Andy Thomson)

(Below)
Even from the two-seat variant of the F-16 the pilot has an excellent view from the raised cockpit, which is evident in this shot of F-16D 84-323 'LF'. The yellow fin band denotes the aircraft is from 314th FS 'Warhawks', 58th FW.

(Right)
When F-16s began to arrive at Shaw AFB, South Carolina in 1985 to replace the RF-4C Phantoms the result was a change in the Wing designation, becoming the 363rd Tactical Fighter Wing. This also included a change of tailcode from 'JO' to the more appropriate 'SW'. The 363rd comprises three squadrons; the 17th, 19th and 33rd, all initially received F-16As, but have since upgraded to the C model. The USAF restructuring programme has meant a further designation change for the Wing, which is now simply a Fighter Wing. Illustrated is 17th FS F-16C 84-253 'SW' with the squadron name 'Hooters' on the fin.

(Below)
The 363rd TFW played a major part in the ground offensive during operation Desert Storm, and the major theme at the 1991 London (Ontario) International Air Show was a Desert Storm tribute. Appropriately the 19th TFS 'Gamecocks' sent a couple of aircraft to the show, including F-16C 89-004 'SW' marked as the squadron commander's aircraft.

The final Stateside front line Wing to receive the F-16 was the 347th TFW at Moody AFB, Georgia which began to dispose of its F-4E Phantoms in 1985. The Wing's three squadrons, the 68th 'Lightning Lancers', 69th 'Dragons' and 70th 'White Knights' have completed conversion to the F-16C from their earlier A models. The Wing was due to deactivate in 1993 with the closure of its base – a consequence of glasnost. However this decision has been rescinded, and the Wing has in fact increased in size, though this has been due to the need to find a home for aircraft forced to flee Homestead and Hurricane Andrew. Two Homestead units, the 307th and 308th FS are currently attached to Moody until a decision has been made on the future of the Florida base. One of the 68th TFS F-16As 83-098 'MY' was photographed whilst participating in a Maple Flag exercise at CFB Cold Lake in May 1989.

The first Wing outside the US to receive F-16s was the famous 8th TFW 'Wolf Pack' of Vietnam fame which disposed of its Phantoms and received its first F-16As in September 1981. The Wing's aircraft carry a wolf's head on the fin alongside the obvious 'WP' tailcode, as seen in this shot of an 80th TFS 'Headhunters' F-16A.

UNITED STATES AIR FORCE PACIFIC AIR FORCES (PACAF)

From its headquarters at Hickam AFB Hawaii, PACAF controls four numbered Air Forces, the 3rd AF in Japan, 7th AF in the Republic of Korea, the 11th AF at Elmendorf, Alaska and 13th AF in Guam. The latter used to reside at Clark AB in the Philippines until the US withdrew from that base. PACAF currently has three F-16 Wings; the 8th FW at Kunsan AB and 51st Wing at Osan AB, Korea and the 432nd FW at Misawa, Japan. There is also a single Fighter Squadron, the 18th at Eielson under the 343rd Wing. PACAF also controlled, briefly, the 26th Aggressor Squadron under the 18th TFW at Kadena. The squadron previously operated the F-5E at Clark, but moved to Kadena in readiness to receive five F-16Cs. Whilst the unit's personnel were busy settling in at Kadena the squadron's aircraft were temporarily assigned to the 51st at Osan; however before the aircraft could be delivered to their intended owners the USAF announced it was curtailing its aggressor squadron activities, and the 26th AS disbanded before it had received its aircraft!

The 8th FW is based at Kunsan AB on the west coast of South Korea and shares the base with a squadron of RoKAF F-5Es. The Wing comprises the 35th FS 'First to Fight' with blue fin tips and 80th FS 'Headhunters' with yellow fin tips, and in late 1987 upgraded to the F-16C. The accompanying photograph shows an aircraft from each squadron outside a hardened aircraft shelter at Kunsan in March 1987 when the units were still known as Tactical Fighter Squadrons.

(Right)
Like all operational Wings, each squadron at Kunsan has at least two two-seat variants on strength for training and proficiency purposes. Aircraft 82-1026 'WP' is an F-16B from Kunsan's 35th TFS. Note that the concrete has brown stripes painted on it – most of the paved surfaces at Kunsan are painted in this way which, from a height, apparently gives a paddy-field effect, thereby hoping to fool potential aggressors.

(Below)
This photograph was taken soon after the arrival of F-16Cs at Kunsan, and shows aircraft 86-207 'WP' of the 35th TFS. (Peter Foster)

In the absence of sufficient hardened shelters Kunsan Air Base utilises steel walled revetments filled with sand and earth to help protect its aircraft from surprise attack from South Korea's belligerent neighbour across the 36th Parallel. Note that this 80th TFS F-16A (80-554) has the wolf's head motif behind the cockpit instead of on the fin.

(Above)
Specially marked for the Wing commander and wearing the colours of both squadrons, F-16A 81-708 'WP' was 7th Air Force's solo display aircraft for 1986, and was photographed performing at the Indonesia Air Show at Jakarta's Kemayoran airport in 1986.

(Right)
Located at the stategically important base of Misawa in northern Japan is the 432nd FW which was activated as a Tactical Fighter Wing in July 1985. Initially the Wing had just one squadron, the 13th 'Panthers' equipped with F-16As. The Wing adopted the tailcode 'MJ' for Misawa Japan, as seen on F-16B 83-173.

(Left)
When first formed the 13th TFS had black and white checks on the fin tips, this has since been changed to red. F-16A 83-098 'MJ' is seen landing at Misawa.

(Below)
With air-brakes extended 13th TFS F-16A 83-109 'MJ' makes a perfect landing at Misawa on a beautiful autumn day in 1986. Misawa is a joint USAF/USN/ JASDF base, with a USN P-3 Orion squadron in residence on a rotation basis, usually from Barbers Point, Hawaii. The JASDF elements include 601 Hikotai with Grumman E-2C Hawkeyes, 3 and 8 Hikotai with Mitsubishi F-1 ground-attack aircraft, and a T-33 flight. Due to its remote northerly location and cold winters, a USAF rescue helicopter squadron has recently been activated at the base.

After only a couple of years operating the F-16A, the 13th TFS re-equipped with the C model and, at the same time, changed their squadron colour to red. Wearing special markings for the squadron commander 13th TFS F-16C 86-0234 'MJ' climbs out of Misawa into the dark skies.

(Above)
The 432nd TFW activated a second squadron, the 14th, in late 1986 and, unlike its sister unit the 13th, this squadron was equipped from the outset with the F-16C. The unit's first aircraft, 85-1414 'MJ' in the markings of the squadron commander, looks immaculate in the early morning sunshine at Hickam AFB, Hawaii where it was photographed on its delivery flight. The yellow and black checks on the fin have since been changed to yellow only.

(Left)
With the gear retracting 14th TFS F-16C 85-549 'MJ' takes-off from Misawa.

Another former Phantom unit now equipped with F-16s is the 36th FS 'Flying Fiends' of the 51st FW at Osan AB South Korea. The squadron received its first F-16Cs in January 1989 which adopted the 'OS' tailcode previously worn by the unit's F-4Es, though unfortunately, to date they have not adopted the shark's teeth markings also worn by the Phantoms. The Wing's 25th FS operates the A-10A, and although it was expected to equip with the electric jet there seems no sign of this in the near future. Marked up for the Wing commander whilst still designated a TFW is F-16C 87-251 'OS' with the unit's galloping horse logo. *(Maurice Bertrand)*

UNITED STATES AIR FORCES EUROPE (USAFE)

Until 1982 USAFE was predominantly an F-4 Phantom force with six Wings operating the type, however in July of that year Hahn's 50th TFW set the trend by converting to the F-16, to be followed later by the 52nd TFW at Spangdahlem and the 86th TFW at Ramstein, all under the control of the 17th Air Force. Meanwhile under the 16th Air Force in Spain the 401st TFW also converted from the Phantom to the F-16, and finally under the UK based 3rd Air Force, the 527th Aggressor Squadron (AS) converted from the F-5E to the F-16. A decade later glasnost has taken hold and the 50th TFW has deactivated and Hahn AB closed, whilst in Spain the 401st was deactivated, though this was due more to Spanish political opposition to a foreign military presence on its soil. The Bentwaters based 527 AS also disbanded after a brief career, though the remaining German-based units continue to receive the latest models. Spangdahlem is currently in the process of disposing of its priceless F-4G 'Wild Weasel' Phantoms and will become solely an F-16 Wing.

The 50th TFW comprised three squadrons; the 10th, 313th and 496th which were initially equipped with the F-16A, before conversion to the more capable C model which began towards the end of 1985. The 10th TFS identified its aircraft with a blue band at the top of the fin. The aircraft seen here, F-16A 81-738 'HR' is a 10th TFS aircraft, however it is sporting the colours of all three of the Wing's squadrons for participation in a Gunsmoke competition at Nellis AFB, Nevada.

The white fin stripe on F-16A 80-563 'HR'
identifies it as belonging to the 313th TFS
'Bulldogs'. However upon receiving the F-
16Cs the fin-tip colour was changed to
orange.

(Left)
These two 313th TFS F-16As begin a formation take-off at Greenham Common for a flight back to their Hahn base.

(Below)
On a rare sunny winter's day in the UK F-16A 80-561 'HR' of the 496th TFS 50th TFW approaches Alconbury. The clean configuration of the aircraft suggests it has been engaged in DACT training with the locally-based F-5Es of the 527th AS.

(Right)
Seen at the 1988 Mildenhall Air Fête is 496 TFS F-16C 84-299 'HR'. Note that the squadron has changed its fin-tip colour to gold from the red worn on its A models.

(Below)
At the sprawling Torrejon AB on the outskirts of Madrid the 401st TFW converted from the F-4D to the F-16A in 1983. All three squadrons, the 612th, 613th and 614th subsequently upgraded to the F-16C. The Wing took part in offensive operations during operation Desert Storm, including operations from Incirlik in Turkey. Due to political pressure from the Spanish Government which wanted the removal of foreign forces from its territory, the Wing planned to move to Crotone in Italy, however, the Wing in fact disbanded and aircraft transferred. Illustrated is 612th TFS F-16A 82-988 'TJ' on final approach to Alconbury. This squadron was the second in the Wing to disband, and did so in October 1991.

Aircraft of the 401st TFW were infrequent visitors to the UK, however F-16A 83-079 'TJ' of the 613th TFS was snapped during a visit to Alconbury in January 1985. This squadron was disbanded on 28 June 1991.

(Right)
A rare event — a year after equipping on the type three Torrejon aircraft visit RAF Leuchars, one aircraft from each squadron. Nearest the camera is F-16A 82-904 'TJ' of the 614th, whilst behind are aircraft from the 613th and 612th.

(Below)
Ramstein's 86th TFW was the first USAFE unit to equip with the F-16C variant, and did so at the end of 1985. F-16C 84-286 was chosen as the Wing commander's aircraft and, rather unusually for a period seemingly obsessed with camouflaging everything that moved, the aircraft appeared with a candy striped red and white tail.

(Above)
Long-time home to the Phantom, Ramstein transferred its 'RS' tailcode to the F-16s, the first of which were delivered to the 512th TFS 'Dragons'. F-16C 85-454 displays the unit's green and black fin stripes.

(Left)
The 526th TFS transitioned from the F-4E to the F-16C early in 1986 and within eighteen months had traded-in those aircraft for ones powered by General Electric engines. Photographed inbound to Lakenheath is 85-402 'RS'.

The red and black fin stripe markings identify F-16C 85-408 'RS' as a 526th FS 'Black Knights' machine. The 86th also comprises transport assets and is therefore designated 86th Wing instead of Fighter Wing.

(Above)
Spangdahlem's 52nd TFW was the final USAFE F-16 unit to form and did so with the C model on 4 July 1987. The role of the F-16 in the 52nd is unique in the USAF in that the electric jet operates alongside the F-4G 'Wild Weasel' Phantoms in the SAM suppression role. At the time of writing however the F-4s are in the process of returning Stateside, and the 52nd will be an F-16 Wing only. Sporting sharks-teeth markings, F-16C 87-270 'SP' is the aircraft assigned to the wing commander, which sports the colours of all three squadrons at the top of the fin.

(Left)
The second squadron within the 52nd TFW is the 81st TFS, a long time operator of the F-4G. When the 52nd was a Phantom Wing the 81st initially operated all the 'Wild Weasel' G models, whilst the two other squadrons, the 23rd and 480th, flew the F-4E variant. On static display at the 1988 Mildenhall Air Fete is 81st TFS F-16C 86-270 'SP'.

F-16D 85-572 'SP' belongs to the 480th TFS, and is seen making a perfect landing at Fairford. Unlike the aircraft of some export customers, USAF Fighting Falcons do not have a brake parachute to aid deceleration after landing, the alternative is to hold the nose of the aircraft high and use aerodynamic braking.

The hunters prowl! A 480th TFS F-16C escorts an F-4G from the same unit. The 52nd TFW is unique in operating both types alongside each other. This F-16C is carrying a Westinghouse ALQ-131 ECM pod on the centreline pylon. Both the F-4G and F-16C use AGM-45 Shrike and AGM-88 HARM missiles to knock-out enemy radar and SAM sites. (*Author's collection*)

(Above)

The final and shortest lived USAFE F-16 unit was the 527th Aggressor Squadron which used to operate the F-5E Tiger II as a component of Alconbury's 10th TRW. The squadron moved to the 81st TFW at Bentwaters and took delivery of its first F-16Cs in January 1989. Seen inside its hardened shelter at Bentwaters is F-16C 86-229 wearing the 81st TFW 'WR' tail-code.

(Right)

The USAF's decision to disband its aggressor squadron came as something of a surprise to most people. These squadrons were formed in light of the experience in Vietnam where a study found that most pilots who were shot down were inexperienced and usually in the early stages of their tour of duty. The task of the aggressor squadrons was to give the average squadron pilot combat-type experience. During the 1980s the aggressor squadrons proved very popular with units queueing up to participate in air combat training missions. The aggressors were disbanded as an economy measure – a decision felt by many, myself included, to be false economy. Wearing Soviet-style fighter codes on the fuselage 527th AS F-16C 86-231 'WR' was photographed on approach to Lakenheath shortly before the unit disbanded in October 1990.

UNITED STATES AIR FORCE
AIR NATIONAL GUARD (ANG)

The Air National Guard has the distinction of being the largest F-16 operator in the world, with more aircraft and units than the regular US Air Force. At the time of writing there are thirty-five squadrons operating the type, with at least a further five planned to convert within the next year. It is now quite common for the Guard to receive modern equipment straight from the production line. This was not always so however, as until the nineteen-eighties the Guard was the recipient of aircraft handed down from the regular Air Force, usually as those aircraft approached obsolescence. The Air National Guard, often known as weekend warriors is largely made up of reservists who have a commitment to train for a certain number of days per year. Not unnaturally, many pilots do in fact fly for airlines, and on their days off fly for the Guard. Many previously served in the regular Air Force before joining an airline, and now have the contrast of perhaps

flying a B747 one day, and on F-16 the next! Not all Guard pilots fly professionally however, many are from other professions, such as doctors, dentists, accountants etc. Of the groundcrews and support staff, less tend to have seen regular service, though a number are full-time Guard personnel. This system proves ideal with long-term stability and continuity, hence aircraft assigned to Guard units tend to have superior serviceability records than their regular Air Force counterparts, and the aircraft are generally maintained to an excellent standard. The ANG units are part funded by the State where they are located and serve, and there is at least one Guard unit in each State. Each ANG base is organised such that it can operate as an independent unit, though in time of mobilisation units would report to a regular Air Force command, fighter units to Air Combat Command, transport units to Air Mobility Command etc.

Arizona ANG's 148th TFTS received its first F-16s early in 1986. As a component of the 162nd TFG based at Tucson the unit's task is to train pilots for ANG and AFRES F-16 equipped squadrons. As a training unit the squadron naturally has a number of two-seat F-16B models on strength, including 79-417 illustrated here.

With an AIM-9 Sidewinder missile on the starboard wing tip F-16A 80-607 of Arizona's 148th TFTS heads for home at the end of a training mission. (*Peter Foster*)

(Left)
Within the 162nd TFG there were two squadrons equipped with the A-7D/K Corsair; the 152nd and 195th. Both how-ever have now converted to the F-16A alongside the 148th. At present there are no plans for these units to upgrade to the F-16C, and they are likely to retain their A models for the time being. F-16A 78-056 is an early-build A model of the 148th TFTS and was photographed at London (Ontario).

(Below)
The state of the District of Columbia has its own fighter unit in the shape of the 113th FW's 121st FS. However, as there is no air base located in the tiny state, the unit is based at Andrews AFB, Maryland, in the suburbs of Washington DC. One of the unit's F-16As is seen taxiying for a training mission.

The 121st FS D.C. ANG has a long tradition as a fighter squadron, from the P-47 Thunderbolts it operated immediately after the Second World War, to the F-100 Super Sabre, F-105 Thunderchief and finally the F-4D Phantom. It received the F-16A model in 1990. Adorned with the squadron's 'DC' tailcode, F-16A 79-344 sits at the holding point waiting for his wingman to complete his last chance checks.

A DC ANG F-16A on final approach to one of Andrew's long parallel runways.

(Right)
In the era of toned-down markings only the aircraft assigned to the squadron commander wears high visibility colour markings, which for the 121st FS are red. The others, like 79-344 'DC' have the fin-tip markings in a less conspicuous grey.

(Below)
Florida ANG's 159th Fighter Interceptor Squadron (FIS), 125th Fighter Interceptor Group (FIG) became the first Air National Guard unit to operate the F-16 dedicated to the air defence role when it received the type towards the end of 1986, replacing the F-106 Delta Dart. Wearing the unit's blue fin band and white lightning flash is F-16A 80-565, parked alongside an F-106A which it replaced. These colourful markings have since been replaced by a low visibility two-tone grey version. The unit designation is now 159th FS 125th FG.
(Duncan MacIntosh)

Like many front line units a high percentage of Air National Guard squadrons operated the F-4 Phantom prior to receiving the F-16; one such unit is the 170th TFS, 183rd TFG Illinois ANG. Based at Springfield's Capitol Airport the squadron is equipped with the A model in the ground-attack role. Posing on the Springfield ramp in extremely colourful markings is F-16A 82-953 wearing the unit's 'SI' tailcode. (*Andy Thomson*)

(Right)
In conjunction with just the Tucson-based training units, the 184th FG is also entrusted with the training of pilots for ANG F-16 units. Based at McConnell AFB, Kansas, the Wing comprises two squadrons; the 127th TFS which is operational in the ground-attack role, whilst the 161st is a training squadron. The 161st has just completed conversion from the F-16A to the C model in readiness to train crews for the ANG A-7 and A-10 squadrons about to convert to the General Dynamics fighter. All 184th TFG aircraft carry the words Kansas and the unit's nickname 'Jayhawks' on the fin, as seen on F-16A 80-495.

(Below)
As a training unit the 184th TFG naturally has a large number of two-seat variants on strength; illustrated is F-16B 80-624 with a Mark 82 bomb on the port outer pylon.

Selfridge AFB on the outskirts of Detroit, Michigan is home to two ANG F-16A units. The first to receive the 'electric jet' was the 107th TFS 127th TFW which began converting from the A-7D in early 1990. The squadron's first couple of aircraft appeared with large unit insignia on the fin as seen on aircraft 80-505 which was photographed in June 1990 at the London (Ontario) Air Show. Sadly, the squadron was instructed by higher command to reduce the size of the insignia, which is now a fraction of its former size.

(Above)
Also at Selfridge, but tasked with air defence, is the 171st FIS, 191st FIG of the Michigan ANG. The unit disposed of its F-4D Phantoms in favour of the F-16A in mid 1990, following the conversion of its sister unit, the 107th TFS. In its Phantom days the 171st had one of the most colourful markings around with black and yellow checks covering much of the fin. Sadly these have toned-down to the now familiar two-tone grey version, as on F-16A 80-579. Under the USAF unit reorganisation Fighter Interceptor Squadrons are now designated Fighter Squadrons.

(Right)
Note that 171st FIS aircraft also have the checker-board markings above the intake. In the background are 107th TFS aircraft with reduced size squadron insignia.

(Left)
F-16As assigned to Air National Guard air defence squadrons are being modified to F-16A (ADF) standard. The ADF stands for Air Defense Fighter, and 270 aircraft are earmarked for such conversion, which includes provision to carry AIM-7 Sparrow and AIM-120 AMRAAM missiles, improved radar, IFF and communications. These aircraft are also being fitted with a searchlight located just aft of the nose-cone to assist in visual identification during night intercepts. Though devoid of markings, this F-16A (ADF) 82-945 belongs to Michigan's 171st FIS, 191st FIG. The ADF variant can be identified by the bulge at the base of the fin which houses the HF radio equipment, also note the searchlight aft of the nose-cone.

(Below)
Unmarked 171st FIS F-16A 81-708 makes a steep climbing turn with full afterburner.

(Above)
One of the last units to dispose of its F-106 Delta Darts was the 186th FIS, 120th FIG Montana ANG. Based at Great Falls the unit now operates the F-16A (ADF) and is a vital component of North American Air Defense Command (NORAD). Not yet converted to ADF standard, 80-563 formates with a KC-135 tanker to wait his turn on the boom. (Peter Foster)

(Right)
Formerly an A-10 unit New York ANG's 138th TFS, 174th TFW operates the F-16A model from its base at Syracuse. The squadron began converting to its current mount in November 1988 and became the first F-16 squadron dedicated to the close air support role. For these missions the very effective GPU-5A Pave Claw 30mm gun pod is carried on the centre-line pylon. The squadron excelled in this role during operation Desert Storm. The unit is known as 'The Boys from Syracuse' and is allocated the appropriate 'NY' tailcode. F-16A 79-403 'NY' taxies past the Canadian 'Snowbirds' aerobatic team on arrival at London (Ontario) for the F-16 meet at the 1990 Air Show. The squadron converted to the F-16C model during 1993/94.

Within the state of New York air defence is provided by the Air National Guard's 136th FIS, 107 FIG. Based at Niagara Falls Airport, the squadron previously operated the F-101 Voodoo and F-4D Phantom before converting to the F-16A (ADF) in late 1990. Displaying the unit's revised tail markings, F-16A (ADF) 80-547 approaches the famous Niagara Falls from the Canadian side of the border. Unfortunately the sight of 'electric jets' over this famous landmark is now a rare occurrence, as the unit converted to the KC-135R Stratotanker during 1994. *(136th FIS)*

(Above)
The training of pilots destined for ANG air defence squadrons is the task of the 114th FS, 142nd FG Oregon ANG based at Kingsley Field, Klamath Falls. The group also has an operational F-15A unit, the 123rd FS at Portland. The 114th disposed of its F-4C Phantoms in 1989 in favour of the F-16A and shortly afterwards began to receive the first ADF versions converted. Adorned with the squadron's giant eagle insignia is F-16A(ADF) 81-811. Note the searchlight just aft of the nose-cone and bulge at the base of the fin which identify this as an ADF variant. When Air Education and Training Command was activated on 1 July 1993 it assumed responsibility from Air Combat Command for this unit, and the training units at McConnell and Tucson.

(Right)
The distinction of being the first Air National Guard unit to equip with the F-16 fell to the South Carolina ANG's 157th TFS 169th TFG at McEntire ANGB. Formerly an A-7D unit the squadron received its first F-16As in mid 1983, and these are used in the ground-attack role. The squadron was upgraded to active duty status for operation Desert Storm where the squadron fought alongside New York ANG's 138th TFS. Five aircraft from the 157th are seen in echelon. Note the squadron 'Swamp Fox' logo behind the cockpit. (Don Spering/A.I.R.)

UNITED STATES AIR FORCE – AIR FORCE RESERVE (AFRES)

The Air Force Reserve is a force which concentrates on transport duties and, unlike the Air National Guard has few fighter units. Unlike the Air National Guard the Air Force Reserve has no commitments to the State they are based in, and its F-16 units are also dual role, leaving the air defence task to the Guard units. As with many Guard units the Reserve has been in the process of upgrading units with more modern equipment, and currently has eight squadrons of F-16s, three of which now operate the C model.

The first AFRES unit to receive the F-16 was the 466th TFS, 419th TFW at Hill AFB, Utah which hosts the 388th TFW, the USAF's first F-16 Wing. The 466th 'Diamondbacks' was the last operator of the F-105D Thunderchief, and received its first F-16As way back in January 1984. The squadron's association with Hill AFB is signified by the 'HI' tailcode, as seen on F-16A 78-066. The aircraft was photographed at George AFB in 1986, and still wears the World Champs logo having won the previous year's Gunsmoke exercise at Nellis AFB.

The first reserve unit to receive the F-16C model was the 302nd TFS, 944th TFG at Luke AFB, Arizona. The unit was previously the 302nd SOS which flew CH-3E helicopters – quite a transition! With the change in equipment came a change of tailcode from 'LH' to 'LR', no doubt standing for Luke Reserves. The squadron nickname is 'Sun Devils', and one of the unit's aircraft is featured over typical inhospitable Arizona terrain. *(General Dynamics)*

In 1989 a further three AFRES squadrons converted to the F-16A, after the 465th TFS at Tinker, Oklahoma, came the 89th TFS of the 906th TFG at Wright-Patterson AFB, Ohio. Another former F-4D Phantom unit the 89th is assigned the 'DO' tailcode for Dayton, Ohio. Wright-Patterson AFB is very close to the metropolis of Dayton, but within the limits of the city of Fairborn, hence the Group Commander's aircraft, 800474 'DO' carries the name *City of Fairborn* on the nose.

One month after the 89th TFS received its first F-16A, the 93rd TFS, 482nd TFW at Homestead AFB, Florida did likewise. Another former Phantom unit the 93rd has an air-ground role, and shared Homestead with the F-16 equipped 31st FW. The squadron managed to escape Hurricane Andrew when it devastated Homestead, and currently resides at McDill AFB. It is believed the unit is to remain there, but with conversion to the KC-135R on the cards. F-16A 820906 'FM' is the aircraft assigned to the squadron commander. (*Andy Thomson*)

UNITED STATES NAVY

The US Navy long ago recognised the value of air combat training and had aggressor units on both east and west coasts equipped with A-4 Skyhawks and F-5E Tiger IIs, and later the F-21 Kafir. The Navy soon realised the F-16's potential for dissimilar air combat training, and announced an order for the type in January 1985. It now has twenty-six aircraft on strength, four of which are the TF-16N two-seat variant. The navalised variant of the F-16 is used purely in the training role as it has no armament or radar. Despite their youth however, Navy F-16Ns are believed to be suffering fatigue problems due to the consistent high G manoeuvres associated with their aggressor task. There are currently four Naval units operating the F-16N; the Naval Fighter Weapons School and VF-126 at Miramar, California, VF-43 at Oceana, Virginia and VF-45 at Key West, Florida.

The first unit to receive the F-16N was VF-126 'Bandits' at NAS Miramar, where the type supplements elderly TA-4J Skyhawks in providing DACT against F-14 Tomcat squadrons assigned to the Pacific Fleet. One of the unit's aircraft is illustrated wearing Soviet-style red star and 'NJ601' code. (*Andy Thomson*)

The Naval Fighter Weapons School based at Miramar runs Topgun courses for selected pilots from front line fighter squadrons, as those who have seen the film of the same name will know. The Navy F-16s are painted two shades of light grey which is a very effective camouflage and make the aircraft difficult to spot at altitude. The Navy procured four TF-16N two-seaters, and the machine illustrated; 163279 '46' is assigned to the Naval Fighter Weapons Squadron (NFWS).

(Above)
The Marine Corps also participate in the Topgun programme, providing both students and instructors. To signify this involvement one NFWS F-16N, aircraft 163269 '42' is painted in a grey and green camouflage pattern with Marines titling.

(Left)
Based at NAS Key West at the southern tip of the Florida Keys is VF-45 'Blackbirds'. Like its sister units VF-45 also operates the A-4 and F-5 in the aggressor role and its F-16s have red stars painted on the fin. Wearing the squadron's 'AD' tailcode is one of the unit's F-16Ns on approach to Nellis AFB. (Peter Foster)

The last navy unit to receive the F-16N was VF-43 Challengers at NAS Oceana, where the type is used predominantly for air combat training with F-14 Tomcat units assigned to the Atlantic Fleet. The squadron also operates the A-4E, F-5E and T-2C. Photographed on the Oceana flightline is a VF-43 F-16N wearing the squadron's insignia on the fin. Like VF-45 the unit is allocated the 'AD' tailcode, though it is seldom worn.

EUROPE

As mentioned earlier four European NATO partners; Belgium, Denmark, Netherlands and Norway selected the F-16 to replace their ageing F-104 Starfighters. Two production lines were set up – at Gosselies in Belgium SABCA produced aircraft for the Belgian and Danish Air Forces whilst at Fokker's Schiphol plant aircraft for the Dutch and Norwegian Air Forces were produced. Initial plans called for the production of 116 aircraft for Belgium, fifty-eight for Denmark, 102 for the Netherlands and seventy-two for Norway, however all four countries ordered additional batches. At Gosselies production for Belgium and Denmark has been completed, the totals being 160 and seventy respectively. At Schiphol the Norwegian re-order was for only two aircraft, both of which

were two-seat B models, these taking their total to seventy-four, all of which have been delivered. The Dutch order totals 213 aircraft, delivery of which is near to completion. Subsequently two other European NATO partners, Greece and Turkey have ordered and received the F-16, the former being General Dynamics-built aircraft whilst the Turks built their own plant at Murted near Ankara. One other NATO country, Portugal, received seventeen A and three B models during 1994. These will equip the newly formed 201 Escuadron at Monte Real where they will be employed in the air defence role, thereby releasing the A-7P Corsair to a more traditional anti-shipping/ground attack role.

BELGIUM

The Belgian Air Force (Force Aerienne Belge/Belgische Luchtmacht) ordered an initial batch of ninety-six F-16As and twenty F-16Bs. These replaced the F-104 Starfighter with 349 and 350 Smaldeel (Squadron) of No.1 Wing at Beauvechain, and 23 and 31 Smaldeel of Kleine-Brogel's No.10 Wing. At a later date the Operational Conversion Squadron was established at Beauvechain. More recently at Florennes No.2 Wing received the F-16 to equip numbers 1 and 2 Smaldeel, both former Mirage 5 units. The Belgian Air Force received its first aircraft in January 1979 becoming the first overseas operator of the type. It now has a total of 136 F-16As and twenty-four F-16Bs. Over the past couple of decades the Belgian Air Force has consistently suffered from defence cuts imposed on it by the government, the result being that its pilots fly a considerable number of hours less than the stated NATO minimum. The most recently announced round of

cuts however will have a devastating effect on the Belgian Air Force and the morale of its personnel. The planned avionics upgrade of the sole remaining Mirage V squadron has been halted and the type is to be withdrawn. The F-16 fleet does not escape the axe, as No.1 Wing at Beauvechain was disbanded in 1994, and the base received all the training aircraft; SF260, CM170 and Alpha Jets from Goetsenhoeven and Brustem/St. Truiden, allowing those bases to close. The Beauvechain squadrons are now located thus; the Operational Conversion Squadron and 349 Squadron at No.10 Wing, Kleine-Brogel, with 350 Squadron with No.2 Wing at Florennes, all with a reduced number of aircraft. A number of F-16s are to be stored for wartime reserve, and some may be sold, though the current Chief of Staff is bitterly fighting this decision.

At Beauvechain the Operational Conversion Squadron (OCS) was established as the training unit for all Belgian pilots. This training establishment was originally formed as a flight, and shared the two-seat B models with the Wing's two operational squadrons, 349 and 350. During this period these aircraft were devoid of unit markings. On upgrading to squadron status the OCS received its own aircraft which carry the Tactical Air Force yellow eagle within a blue band outlined in red. Displaying such markings is F-16B FB-10 lined-up for departure at Beauvechain.

No.2 Wing at Florennes was the last
Belgian Wing to equip with the F-16
and comprises numbers 1 and 2 Smaldeel
(Squadrons), both of which previously
operated the Mirage 5BA. Aircraft of both
squadrons carry the Wing's black and
white diamond insignia within a coloured
band at the top of the fin, this band being
black outlined in yellow for 1 Smaldeel,
and blue outlined in white in the case of 2
Smaldeel. Both squadrons also display
their own insignia; a black thistle for 1
Smaldeel and a red shooting-star for 2
Smaldeel. Illustrated is F-16A FA-118 of
the latter unit.

(Left)
Kleine-Brogel Air Base near the Dutch border is home to 10 Wing's 23 and 31 Smaldeel which operate in the strike/attack role. The Wing received its F-16s after the Beauvechain units had equipped and aircraft of both squadrons carry the Wing's red lion rampant within a blue shield on the fin, as seen on F-16B FB-01. This aircraft was Belgium's first two-seater and was photographed on a visit to RAF Brawdy.

(Below)
Aircraft of 23 Smaldeel can be identified by the unit insignia of a devil's head within a red and white fin stripe. F-16A FA-95 is seen at RAF Leuchars where the aircraft performed at the annual Battle of Britain Air Show in 1989.

(Above)
The other component of 10 Wing is 31 Smaldeel, one of the founder members of the NATO Tiger Squadron Meet. Like all members of this exclusive club the unit proudly displays its tiger insignia on the fin. A four-ship formation of 31 Smaldeel aircraft are seen here at low level somewhere over Belgium. (Peter Foster)

(Right)
Aircraft of 10 Wing normally make use of Helchteren Range, a short distance and a few minutes flying time from their Kleine Brogel base, however during NATO exercises ranges in other allied countries are often used. Screaming in low and fast and about to drop some ordnance on the RAF range at Holbeach on The Wash is 31 Smaldeel F-16A FA-88.

At Beauvechain No.1 Wing's 349 Smaldeel became operational in January 1981, and was the first operational F-16 unit outside the US. Like its sister unit 350 Smaldeel, 349 operates in the air defence role. The unit insignia is a pair of spiked chained balls (known as Goedendag) within a blue fin stripe outlined in white. This pair of 349 Smaldeel aircraft were photographed during a visit to RAF Brawdy.

(Above)
To commemorate the unit's 45th anniversary 349 Smaldeel painted F-16A FA-49 in special markings with giant-sized unit insignia across the aircraft's spine. (Heribert Mennen)

(Right)
Flaring for a perfect landing at Beauvechain is FA-22, an F-16A of 350 Smaldeel. The unit insignia comprises the yellow head of Ambiorix within a red fin band.

DENMARK

The Royal Danish Air Force (Kongelige Danske Flyvevaaben) ordered an initial batch of forty-six F-16As and twelve F-16Bs, initially to replace the elderly F-100D Super Sabres of Eskadrilles (Squadrons) 727 and 730 at Skrydstrup, and later the F-104G Starfighters of Eskadrilles 723 and 726 at Aalborg. A follow-on order for a further eight F-16As and four F-16Bs were received from the Fokker production line at Schiphol. Like Belgium, the Danish have also suffered recent defence cuts, and the fleet of

Saab 35 Draken ground-attack aircraft have recently been withdrawn from service, though the reconnaissance variant remains operational. For those historians interested in dates, Eskadrille 727 became an F-16 unit on 1 July 1980, and was declared operational on the 1 April 1981. Eskadrille 730 officially began transition to the F-16 on 1 January 1981, with Eskadrille 723 following on the 1 January 1983. The final unit, Eskadrille 726 completed conversion during 1986.

(Left)
Danish F-16 operators carry minute squadron markings usually on the port side of the intake, the exception is 726 Eskadrille who display their insignia, a red shield with a silver triple claw motif upon it. Based at Aalborg, 726 was the final Danish unit to receive the F-16 which it employs in the air defence role. Above the solid clouds F-16B ET-614 displays the 726 Eskadrille insignia on the fin. (Ian Black)
(Below)
The first Aalborg-based, and third Danish unit to receive the F-16 was 723 Eskadrille, whose unit insignia comprises a blue and silver shield with an eagle of the same colours superimposed. Like its sister unit 726, the unit's aircraft are used primarily in the air defence role. Carrying a dayglo red dummy AIM-9J on each wingtip F-16A E-198 departs RAF Waddington with full afterburner.

(Right)
The first Danish unit to receive the F-16 was Eskadrille 727, which did so at Skrydstrup in July 1980. The delivery of the state-of-the-art 'electric jet' was quite a contrast, as the unit was until then operating the elderly but much loved F-100D Super Sabre, better known to enthusiasts and pilots alike as the Sled. With airbrakes extended, F-16A E-199 demonstrates a slow high angle of attack flypast at the 1988 Mildenhall Air Fête. The squadron insignia is a silver Thor's hammer and gold lightning flashes on a blue shield.

(Below)
Seen in a tight turn over a Danish lake is F-16A E-174 from Skrydstrup's Eskadrille 730. The unit began conversion to its current mount in January 1981 having previously flown the F-100D. The unit was initially tasked with converting pilots to the F-16, but now has a fully operational role.

GREECE

The Hellenic Air Force (Elliniki Aeroporia) is one of the more recent customers for the F-16, and received the first of thirty-four F-16Cs and six D models towards the end of 1988. These equip two units, 330 and 346 Moira (Squadron) of No.111 Pterix (Wing) at Nea Anghialos Air Base. These units were activated to operate the F-16s, with 330 having a primary air defence role and secondary ground-attack role, sister unit 346 Moira has the priorities reversed. The Wing also has a single F-5A squadron which, surprisingly is assigned air defence duties. The Greeks are almost certain to purchase additional aircraft to re-equip at least this F-5 squadron, and an order for a further batch of forty is believed to be imminent, particularly in view of the fact that the Turks have a large number of the type. The Hellenic Air Force does not permit first tour personnel to fly the F-16s, therefore all pilots selected to fly the type are experienced, having previously flown the F-4, F-5, F-104 or Mirage F1. This system undoubtedly pays off as, at the time of writing after four years of operating the type, they have not lost a single aircraft.

Greek F-16s are finished in a two-tone matt grey camouflage scheme and carry no national insignia on the fuselage, only the Greek flag on the fin. They are also devoid of unit markings. Illustrated is F-16D 144.

A pair of F-16Cs of 346 Moira lined up for
take-off at Nea Anghialos.

THE NETHERLANDS

The Royal Netherlands Air Force (Koninklijke Luchtmacht) is the largest F-16 operator outside the US. The first order was for 102 aircraft but subsequent orders in 1980 and 1989 have taken the total to 213, comprising thirty-six F-16Bs and 177 F-16As, all but a few of which have been delivered. First deliveries were in June 1979, and soon equipped former Starfighter squadrons; 306, 311 and 312 at Volkel, and 322 and 323 at Leeuwarden, as well as a training unit at the latter base. Later deliveries went to 313 and 315 Squadrons at Twenthe, 314 at Gilze-Rijen and 316 at Eindhoven, all of these being former NF-5 units. The Leeuwarden-based training unit has since disbanded, and training is now undertaken with the Arizona Air National Guard at Tucson, where the Dutch have a batch of aircraft assigned and which operate in US markings. On completion of training at Tucson, pilots join 316 Squadron at Eindhoven for training in a European environment. No.316 disbanded in 1994, and 314 will move to Leeuwarden in 1996. The Dutch will also acquire three ex Martinair DC-10s which will be converted to tanker/cargo/passenger configuration. This important acquisition will provide the force with its first air-refuelling tankers, and they will no longer have to rely on USAF KC-135s being made available for air refuelling training and assistance in deployments. To help offset operating costs, the aerial refuelling assets of the DC-10s will almost certainly be made available to the other European F-16 operators, particularly neighbours Belgium and Denmark.

For a short while the TCA (Transitie en Conversie Afdeling) at Leeuwarden was responsible for training Dutch pilots but the unit was disbanded in March 1986 when the training syllabus was changed. The unit marking was of a shark-like cartoon figure within a blue disc, as seen on F-16A J-215.

The task of tactical reconnaissance within the Netherlands Air Force falls to Volkel's 306 Squadron, which previously used RF-104G Starfighters equipped with the Orpheus pod. The same pod is used with the F-16s and the squadron frequently operates from nearby De Peel, its wartime operational base. With an Orpheus pod on the centreline pylon, F-16A J-637 taxies for departure at Volkel. The squadron badge is an eagle's head on a circle divided vertically, one side blue, the other black containing stars, signifying day and night.

(Left)
All Dutch squadrons have one or two F-16Bs on strength. This aircraft, J-654, belongs to 311 Squadron at Volkel where, along with 312 Squadron, it is tasked with the strike/attack role. The squadron insignia is an eagle on a blue background.

(Below)
To celebrate the 75th anniversary of the Royal Netherlands Air Force in 1988, 312 Squadron painted F-16A J-864 in special markings to commemorate the event. The application of these markings meant that the squadron's crossed swords and red lightning bolt insignia had to be moved from the tail to the ventral fin.

(Above)
Formerly the NF-5 training unit, No.313 Squadron at Twenthe now operates the F-16 in the ground-attack role. Since this photograph of aircraft J-146 was taken the unit has changed its insignia to a tiger's head, thus qualifying for 'Tiger' squadron status.

(Right)
No.314 Squadron used to operate the NF-5 from Eindhoven but, on equipping with the F-16, it relocated to nearby Gilze-Rijen. The squadron received its first F-16 early in 1990 when aircraft J-204 was photographed wearing the unit's golden centaur insignia. (*Author's collection*)

The first Dutch NF-5 unit to convert to the F-16 was 315 Squadron at Twenthe. The squadron's yellow lion's head insignia has been toned down and now appears in low visibility two-tone grey. F-16A J-063 was photographed landing at Fairford to attend the 1989 International Air Tattoo.

(Above)
Dutch F-16s are frequent and welcome visitors to air shows throughout Europe. The unit selected to provide the aircraft for the season usually produces a colourful paint scheme and fits the aircraft with smoke generators. No.315 Squadron did just that with F-16A, J-060 seen performing at RAF Brawdy in 1990.

(Right & Far Right)
Special and anniversary paint schemes are becoming a regular event in Holland, when it seems that never a year goes by without at least one unit falling to the artist's brush. The year 1993 saw the fortieth anniversary of Eindhoven's 316 Squadron. To commemorate the event three of the unit's aircraft were applied with the special tail marking of the head of a bird of prey. Only the eagle-eyed would note that each bird differed very slightly in colour and appearance.

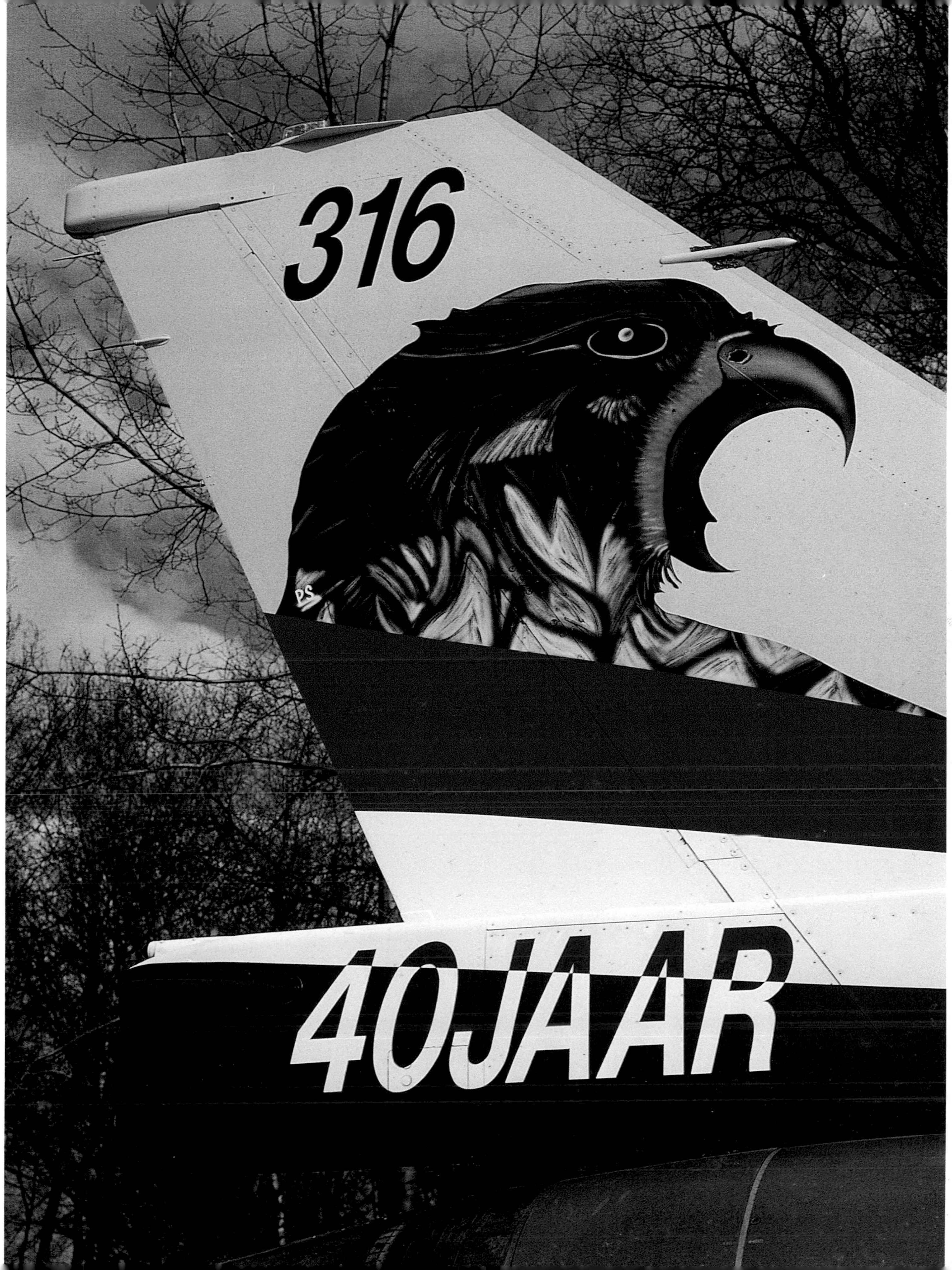
316
40JAAR

(Right)
The first Dutch F-16 unit was 322 Squadron at Leeuwarden which became operational with the type in December 1979 in the air defence role. The unit emblem is 'Polly Grey' the parrot, as seen on F-16B J-260 at RAF Brawdy during a DACT detachment with RAF Hawks of No.1 Tactical Weapons Unit.

(Below)
Two 322 Squadron F-16s, examples of both the A and B model in formation over the North Sea.

To celebrate forty years of 322 Squadron, F-16A J-252 was painted with a bright red fin and large squadron badge. The squadron was formed at Woodvale in 1943 as 322 Squadron RAF and, with a high proportion of Dutch personnel, operated Supermarine Spitfires.

Rotate! No.323 Squadron F-16A J-246 about to leave terra firma on take-off from RAF Brawdy's runway 20. The Leeuwarden-based squadron deployed annually to the Welsh base to conduct DACT missions against the RAF Hawks which, despite being a training aircraft, proved a formidable adversary.

After 322 Squadron, 323 was the next Dutch unit to receive the F-16, and disposed of its F-104G Starfighters in favour of the General Dynamics product in 1980. Seen high over the North Sea near the squadron's Leeuwarden base is F-16B J-270.

(Above)
In addition to the 323 Squadron badge, 'Diana the Hunter', aircraft J-254 also wears the colours of the district of Friesland on the top of the fin. *(Ian Black)*

(Right)
A 323 Squadron F-16B accompanied by a single-seat A model closes astern a USAF KC-135 tanker. Note the refuelling receptacle on the spine behind the cockpit is open in readiness to fill the two 370-gallon underwing fuel tanks.

NORWAY

The Royal Norwegian Air Force (Kongelige Norske Luftforsvaret) ordered sixty F-16As and twelve B models to equip four squadrons; 331 and 334 at Bodo, 332 at Rygge and 338 at Oerland. All these aircraft came from the Fokker production line, and were later followed by two additional F-16Bs as attrition replacements. The two Bodo units previously flew the F-104 Starfighter and 338 the F-5A. One Norwegian unit, 336 Skvadron still operates the F-5 and due to funding difficulties is unlikely to join the F-16 club. Norway's F-16s were the first to feature the extended tail housing which contains a brake parachute for landing on short icy runways, and, like USAF ADF variants have a searchlight in the nose for use on intercepts during the long dark winter days. Conversely, this feature is not required even on night intercepts during the mid-summer months in this land of the midnight sun. Especially those launched from Bodo Air Base which is located north of the Arctic Circle and surrounded by some rugged, yet beautiful scenery. In addition to their air defence task the Norwegians also use the type for ground attack and the anti-shipping role, and for the latter are equipped with the indigenous Penguin anti-ship missile.

(Below)

The Norwegians received their first F-16s in January 1980, and these equipped 332 Skvadron at Rygge, a unit which had been inactive for some five years. The unit initially had a dual role of operational squadron and training unit, and, like 331 Skvadron, was a former RAF unit equipped with Spitfires. Wearing the unit's dark blue and gold pennant on the fin, F-16A number 281 rests on the ramp at Greenham Common.

(Right)
Operating in the air defence role 331 Skvadron was Norway's second F-16 unit when it received the type in late 1981 to replace the F-104G Starfighter. No.331 was formed as an RAF squadron in July 1941 at Catterick, when Norwegian personnel flew the Hawker Hurricane, later being replaced by the Spitfire. The unit has a distinguished wartime record which includes operations from Belgium, France and Holland. No.331 Skvadron aircraft can be identified by the red/white/blue pennant on the fin and blue lightning flash on the forward fuselage

(Below)
Norwegian Air Force aircraft are infrequent visitors to the UK so the appearance of 332 Skvadron F-16A number 276 at the 1988 Mildenhall Air Fête proved very popular with the enthusiasts. The squadron has a dual air defence/ground-attack role and is based at Rygge, a short distance to the south-east of the capital Oslo.

(Above)
Another former Starfighter unit is Bodo's 334 Skvadron which converted to the F-16 in 1982, replacing the ex-Canadian CF-104s which were primarily used in the anti-shipping role. Norwegian F-16s use the locally built Kongsberg Penguin missile for this vital task. Illustrated is F-16B number 693 wearing the squadron's red and white pennant.

(Left)
The final Norwegian F-16 unit to equip with the 'electric jet' was 338 Skvadron based at Oerland, near Trondheim, situated midway between Rygge and Bodo. The unit previously flew the F-5 Freedom Fighter, and squadron markings comprise a yellow lightning bolt within a black pennant, usually backed up by a bow and arrow. About to make a perfect landing is F-16B 307.

TURKEY

Turkey selected the F-16 in 1983 and the type will be used primarily to replace the large fleet of F-104 Starfighters in the Turkish Air Force (Turk Hava Kuvvetleri) inventory. These plans called for the purchase of 160 aircraft, 136 F-16Cs and twenty-four F-16Ds, though the final balance may well change in favour of more two-seaters. Turkey received its first F-16 in October 1987, being one of the batch of eight aircraft built at Fort Worth by General Dynamics. Subsequent aircraft were licence-built by TUSAS Aerospace Industries at a specially constructed plant adjacent to Murted Air Base just south of the capital Ankara. General Dynamics have been extremely impressed by the high quality of the work at TUSAS, who delivered their first aircraft to the Turk Hava Kuvvetleri on 30 November 1987, two months

ahead of schedule. No.4 Ana Jet Us (Main Jet Base) at Murted with F-104Gs was the first base to receive the F-16, equipping 141 and 142 Filo (Squadron) and the training unit, Oncel Filo. The next base to receive the Fighting Falcon was No.6 Ana Jet Us at Bandirma, again replacing ageing F-104G Starfighters, and 162 Filo has already converted, with 161 Filo in the process of doing so. The next unit likely to equip is No.8 Ana Jet Us at Diyarbakir which operates RF-5As and C/F-104s. The Turks have recently ordered another forty F-16s, and further orders are likely to enable the remainder of the fleet of elderly F-5s to be withdrawn, these being with No.5 Ana Jet Us at Merzifon and 133 Filo at Konya.

(*Opposite Page*)
The Turks have an exceptional safety record with the F-16, having lost only one aircraft in over five years of operating the type. The fact that only experienced pilots who have previously flown at least one tour on aircraft such

as the F-4, F-5 or F-104 has obviously played a major part in this. The F-16 training unit is Oncel Filo at Murted, who have a number of two-seat D models on strength, such as 88-0013 seen at rest between missions.

(Above)
All Turkish Air Force aircraft carry their base number and the last three digits of their serial number prominently on the fuselage or nose — except the F-16s. Instead they carry only their aircraft serial number on the fin, as seen on Murted based F-16C 88-0035 turning onto the runway for take-off.

(Above)
On short finals to land at Murted is F-16C 88-0035. The aircraft belongs to 142 Filo, though, as is usual in Turkey, it is unfortunately totally devoid of unit markings.

(Right)
Lined up on Murted's runway in clean configuration is F-16C 86-0069 about to lead a four ship formation for a 2 v 2 air combat training mission. For ground-attack training missions Murted-based aircraft do not have far to travel, after take-off they turn south and join the pattern for the range which is actually within the base perimeter fence.

MIDDLE EAST

The first nation to blood the F-16 in combat was Israel when, on the 7 June 1981, a strike force attacked and badly damaged the Iraqi nuclear reactor at Osirak. Subsequently these aircraft have been involved in strikes against terrorist training camps in Lebanon and occasional skirmishes with Syrian Air Force fighters – all carried out without loss. Israel has a large fleet of F-16s of all models, with further batches of C and D models in the process of being delivered. Israel's former adversary Egypt also has a large number of F-16s on its inventory. Like Israel, the Egyptians operate all four variants, with further C models in the process of being received. Indeed the latest Egyptian order for forty-six aircraft under project 'Peace Vector IV' will be aircraft built by TUSAS at Murted. The only other Middle East nation which operates the F-16 is Bahrain, whose C and D models operate alongside that nation's small fleet of F-5Es.

The tiny Arabian Gulf island state of Bahrain ordered a batch of F-16s in 1987, comprising eight C and four D models. Delivery of these aircraft to the newly built Sheik Isa Air Base was completed in March 1990, and within a year they had been blooded in action with the coalition forces in the war against Iraq. Bahrain is an island roughly the size of the Isle of Man, and the new Sheik Isa Base is located in the barren southern half of the island, well away from the population centres and civil airfield at Muharraq, itself a former RAF base. In full Bahrain Amiri Air Force markings this delightful shot of F-16D number 150 was taken just before the long delivery flight.
(*General Dynamics*)

An early customer for the F-16 was the Israeli Defence Force/Air Force (Heyl Ha'Avir). In 1978 the IDF announced its intention to procure sixty-seven F-16As and eight B models under the project 'Peace Marble'. A batch of B models was initially delivered to Hill AFB, Utah, where the first cadre of Israeli pilots were trained on the type. In October 1987 under 'Peace Marble 2' the first of a batch of seventy-five F-16C/D models were received, whilst a further thirty of each of the latter variants are in the process of being delivered under 'Peace Marble 3'. With the cancellation of its indigenous Lavi fighter in 1987 the F-16 is vital to the security of this small nation surrounded by hostile neighbours. All IDF F-16s are painted in a sand/brown camouflage pattern. Although the F-16 now predominates in the IDF inventory, due to scrupulously strict security few details of operating units are known. Hatzor is known to be an F-16C base, whilst two known F-16 units are supposedly identified as Scorpion Squadron and Valley Squadron, though knowing the Israelis this information may well be a classic case of disinformation! Even in the few photographs which have been released, the squadron markings, where applied, have often been doctored by the censor. Illustrated is an F-16C. (General Dynamics)

ASIA

General Dynamics have been making inroads into the Asian market with the F-16, which is now operated by the air forces of Indonesia, South Korea, Pakistan, Singapore and Thailand. Malaysia had expressed an interest and was at one time expected to receive ex USAF aircraft, however this interest seems to have waned and it appears there are now no plans to procure this type. Japan has also selected the aircraft, a derivative of which will be built by Mitsubishi to serve the Japanese Air Self Defence Force, which is expected to order 130 of the type. First in the region to receive the 'electric jet' was Pakistan when the first of forty F-10A/Bs arrived in the country in January 1983, though as previously mentioned further deliveries were embargoed by the US government. The Republic of (South) Korea was the next customer when it selected the F-16C/D variants. A total of forty of these variants have been delivered, with plans to acquire a further 120, most of which will be built in Korea. Thailand soon followed suit when it procured eighteen F-16A/Bs, and has announced its intention for a further batch of the same number. It was no surprise when in 1985 the air force of Singapore announced its intention to acquire the F-16, albeit in small numbers. Only four A and B models were procured and, although these were received in early 1988, the aircraft remained at Luke AFB where the Singaporian pilots were trained, until January 1990. Indonesia's first F-16s arrived in the archipelago nation in December 1989, and these twelve aircraft now supplement the F-5Es in the air defence role.

The Indonesian Air Force (Tentara Nasional Indonesia Angatan Udara) has a single squadron of F-16s, comprising eight A and four two-seat B models based at Ishwahyudi Air Base, Madiun, on the island of Java. Ishwahyudi is the TNIAU's main fighter base, and is home to number 300 Wing comprising; 11 Skwadron with A-4Es, 14 Skwadron with F-5Es, and the F-16 unit for which no Skwadron number has yet been confirmed. One source has quoted the operating unit as being number 3 Skwadron, with the unit being based at Bacau. Deliveries commenced in December 1989 and were completed within a year. As can be seen in the accompanying photograph, these aircraft are sporting what has to be the most colourful and imaginative camouflage pattern worn by any F-16 operator. (General Dynamics)

(Below)
The Republic of Korea (RoKAF) has a fleet of thirty F-16Cs and ten F-16D models which equip the 161st and 162nd Tactical Fighter Squadrons of the 11th Tactical Fighter Wing at Taegu, where they operate alongside F-4D Phantoms. The first of these was delivered in March 1986. The Korean's plan to build up their own aerospace industry seemed assured when the F-18 Hornet was selected, the majority of which would be built in-country. However, the F-18 programme has now been cancelled and the F-16 selected in its place. A total of 120 aircraft are involved in this ambitious programme. The first twelve aircraft will be built by General Dynamics at Fort Worth, the succeeding thirty-six will be assembled in Korea from US-made components, and the remaining seventy-two will be built in Korea. *(General Dynamics)*

(Above)

Like India, its ongoing adversary, the Pakistani Air Force is well equipped with aircraft from both East and West. The bulk of these are a variety of Chinese-built fighters, the only modern Western combat aircraft being the F-16. The PAF accepted the first of twenty-eight F-16As in October 1982 which, along with twelve F-16Bs were delivered to Sargodha Air Base. A later batch comprising six F-16As and five B models were embargoed by the US, and are currently in store at Davis-Monthan AFB, Arizona. The or-

der for a further sixty aircraft is now in limbo due to a dispute with the US over Pakistan's nuclear policy. At Sargodha a small number of aircraft are used by the Combat Command School, whilst the Operational Conversion Unit is No.11 'Arrows' Squadron. The operational F-16 squadron at Sargodha is No.9 'Griffins', with 14 'Shaheens' Squadron located at Kamra. Pakistan's F-16s were extremely active protecting violations of their airspace from Soviet and Afghan aircraft, and several kills were achieved, most of which were An-26 transport aircraft. One

Pakistani F-16 was lost in combat on 29 April 1987 during an encounter by a pair of F-16s with four Soviet MiG-23s which were bombing guerrilla positions. Although the actual reason for the loss has never been confirmed, the Soviets deny it was shot down. The two most likely theories being that the pilot lost control or consciousness during high G manoeuvres, or that it was hit by bombs raining down on it from the MiGs during their medium-level attack. Photographed landing at Sargodha is 11 Squadron F-16B 82602. (Peter Foster)

(Right)
In April 1985 the Royal Thai Air Force announced its intent to purchase twelve F-16A/Bs, however, by December 1987 when the order was signed the total had been raised to eighteen. These comprised fourteen F-16As and four B models which equip 103 Squadron, No.1 Wing at Korat also known as Nakhon Ratchasima, the former name is certainly more pronounceable! These aircraft are used primarily in the air defence role augmenting Northrop F-5s. The Thai's have recently announced plans for the acquisition of a further batch of eighteen aircraft. With a tiny Thai roundel behind the cockpit and red thunderbolt unit insignia on the fin, 103 Squadron F-16A number 86378 banks over a sparse Thai countryside. (*General Dynamics*)

(opposite page)
In total contrast to the size of the tiny island nation, and the apprehension of its neighbours, the Republic of Singapore Air Force has a considerable number of modern, well-equipped offensive aircraft, including the A-4, F-5, F-16 and Hunter. In comparison to the other types the F-16 force is rather moderate, consisting of four each of the F-16A and B models. These equip No.140 Squadron at the main fighter base, Ten-gah. The first Singaporean aircraft were delivered in February 1988, and these aircraft remained at Luke AFB, Arizona for almost two years whilst pilot training was undertaken. It is understood two of these have been lost already and attrition replacements ordered. The first Singaporean F-16B is illustrated over the US. Note the toned-down national insignia. *(General Dynamics)*

SOUTH AMERICA

To date only one South American nation Venezuela, has selected the F-16. The Venezuelan Air Force (Fuerza Aerea Venezolana) selected the type in 1982 to replace its fleet of Mirage III and Mirage V aircraft, and augment the CF-5s. Total purchase comprised eighteen F-16As and six F-16Bs which have adopted the same brown and two-tone green camouflage scheme worn by the FAV's other combat aircraft. Under project 'Peace Delta' the first of the F-16s was delivered in September 1983, and these aircraft equip two Escuadrones within Grupo Aereo de Caza 16 at El Libertador Air Base; 161 'Caribes' Escuadron and 162 Gavilanes Escuadron. Venezuelan F-16s display the national insignia on the fin and are devoid of unit insignia. Illustrated above is F-16A number 326. *(Peter Foster)*

A USAF F-16C using afterburner at dusk.

ABBREVIATIONS

AB	Air Base
ACC	Air Combat Command
ACF	Air Combat Fighter
ADF	Air Defence Fighter
AE&TC	Air Education & Training Command
AFB	Air Force Base
AFMC	Air Force Materiel Command
AFRES	Air Force Reserve
ANG	Air National Guard
ANGB	Air National Guard Base
AS	Aggressor Squadron
CAS	Close Air Support
CFB	Canadian Forces Base
CTS	Composite Training Squadron
DACT	Disimilar Air Center Training
FAV	Fuerza Aerea Venezolana
FG	Fighter Group
FIG	Fighter Interceptor Group
FIS	Fighter Interceptor Squadron
FIW	Fighter Interceptor Wing
FS	Fighter Squadron
FTS	Fighter Training Squadron
FTS	Flying Training Squadron
FTW	Flying Training Wing
FW	Fighter Wing
FWS	Fighter Weapons Squadron
FWW	Fighter Weapons Wing
IDF	Israeli Defence Force
IFF	Identification Friend or Foe
JASDF	Japanese Air Self Defence Force
NATO	North Atlantic Treaty Organisation
NFWS	Naval Fighter Weapons Squadron
NORAD	North American Air Defense Command
OCS	Operational Conversion Squadron
OCU	Operational Conversion Unit
OG	Operations Group
PACAF	Pacific Air Forces
PAF	Pakistan Air Force
RAF	Royal Air Force
RoCAF	Republic of China Air Force (Taiwan)
RoKAF	Republic of Korea Air Force
TAC	Tactical Air Command
TCA	Transitie de Conversie Afdeling
TEG	Test and Evaluation Group
TES	Test and Evaluation Squadron
TFG	Tactical Fighter Group
TFS	Tactical Fighter Squadron
TFTS	Tactical Fighter Training Squadron
TFTW	Tactical Fighter Training Wing
TFW	Tactical Fighter Wing
TG	Test Group
TNI-AU	Tentara Nasional Indonesia Angatan Udara
TS	Test Squadron
TW	Test Wing
USAAF	United States Army Air Force
USAF	United States Air Force

APPENDIX – F-16 UNITS

N.A.S.A.		F–16A	Langley	

UNITED STATES AIR FORCE – AIR MATERIEL COMMAND

Air Force Flight Test Center

Squadron	Wing	Code	Type	Base
416 TS (ex 6512 TS, 6510TW)	416 TW	'ED'	F-16A-D	Eglin

Air Force Development Test Center

40 TS (ex 3247 TS, 3246 TW)	46 TW	'ET'	F-16A/C	Eglin

Air Logistics Centers

15 TS	Ogden ALC	—	F-16A/B	Hill

UNITED STATES AIR FORCE – AIR EDUCATION AND TRAINING COMMAND

61 FS	56 FW	'LF'	F-16C/D	Luke
62 FS	56 FW	'LF'	F-16C/D	Luke
63 FS	56 FW	'LF'	F-16C/D	Luke
308 FS	56 FW	'LF'	F-16C/D	Luke
309 FS	56 FW	'LF'	F-16C/D	Luke
310 FS	56 FW	'LF'	F-16C/D	Luke
425 FS	56 FW	'LF'	F-16C/D (ex F-16A)	Luke (Singapore training unit)
[63 FS	58 FW]	['LF']	F-16C/D	Luke (ex 56 FW & to 56 FW)
[310 FS	58 FW]	['LF']	F-16C/D	Luke (to 56 FW)

Squadron	Wing	Code	Type	Base
[311 FS	58 FW]	['LF']	F-16C/D	Luke (to 56 FW as 308 FS)
[314 FS	58 FW]	['LF']	F-16C/D	Luke < <DISBANDED> >

(Wing transferred from Air Combat Command 1st July 1993)
(Wing redesignated 56 FW early 1995)

UNITED STATES AIR FORCE – AIR COMBAT COMMAND

USAF Air Warfare Center

85 TS	79 TEG	'OT'	F-16A-D	Eglin

(ex 4485 TS, TAWC)

USAF Weapons and Tactics Centers

'Thunderbirds' 57 FW			F-16C/D	Nellis
			(ex F-16A/B)	
414 CTS	57 OG 57 FW	'WA'	F-16A-D	Nellis
(ex 64 AS)				
422 TES	57 TG 57 FW	'WA'	F-16A-C	Nellis

9th Air Force

77 FS	20 OG 20 FW	'SW'	F-16C	Shaw
78 FS	20 OG 20 FW	'SW'	F-16C	Shaw
79 FS	20 OG 20 FW	'SW'	F-16D	Shaw

(Formerly 17,19, 309 FS, 363 FW. Redesignated 01/01/94)

74 FS	23 WG	'FT'	F-16C	Pope
[306 TFS	31 TFW]	['ZF']	[F-16A]	Homestead < <DISBANDED 31/10/86> >
[307 FS	31 FW]	['HS']	[F-16C] (ex F-16A)	Homestead (to 347 FW)
[308 FS	31 FW]	['HS']	[F-16C] (ex F-16A)	Homestead (ex 'ZF') (to 347 FW)
[309 FS	31 FW]	['HS']	[F-16C] (ex F-16A)	Homestead (ex 'ZF') (to 363 FW)

Due to Hurricane 'Andrew' in 1992 Homestead AFB was virtually destroyed, the three squadrons have been re-assigned as follows; 307 and 308 FS to the 347 FW at Moody AFB, and the 309 FS to the 363 FW at Shaw AFB.

[61 FS	56 OG 56 FW]	['MC']	[F-16C/D] (ex F-16A/B)	McDill < <DISBANDED 12/08/93> >
[62 FS	56 OG 56 FW]	['MC']	[F-16C/D] (ex F-16A/B)	McDill < <DISBANDED 14/05/93> >
[63 FS	56 OG 56 FW]	['MC']	[F-16C/D] (ex F-16A/B)	McDill (to 58 FW)
[72 FS	56 OG 56 FW]	['MC']	[F-16C/D] (ex F-16A/B)	McDill < <DISBANDED 30/06/92> >
68 FS	347 OG 347 WG	'MY'	F-16C (ex F-16A)	Moody
69 FS	347 OG 347 WG	'MY'	F-16C (ex F-16A)	Moody
[70 FS	347 OG 347 WG]	['MY']	[F-16C] (ex F-16A)	Moody < <DISBANDED 1994> >
307 FS	347 OG 347 WG	'MY'	F-16C (ex F-16A)	Moody (ex 31 FW Homestead)
[308 FS	347 OG 347 WG]	['MY']	[F-16C]	Moody (ex 31 FW) < <DISBANDED 1994> >

(redesignated from 347 FW to 347 WG in 1995)

[17 FS	363 OG 363 FW]	['SW']	[F-16C]	Shaw (to 77 FS 20 FW)
[19 FS	363 OG 363 FW]	['SW']	[F-16C]	Shaw (to 78 FS 20 FW)
[27 FS	363 OG 363 FW]	['SW']	[F-16C]	Shaw (to 55 FS and A-10A)
[33 FS	363 OG 363 FW]	['SW']	[F-16C]	Shaw < <DISBANDED 11/06/93> >
[309 FS	363 OG 363 FW]	['SW']	[F-16D]	Shaw (ex 31 FW) (to 79 FS 20 FW))

(Wing redesignated 20 FW 01/01/94)

12th Air Force

Squadron	Wing	Code	Type	Base
522 FS	27 OG 27 FW	'CC'	F-16C	Cannon
(Wing converting from F-111 mid 1995)				
[63 FS	58 FW]	['LF']	[F-16C/D]	Luke (ex 56 FW, to AE&TC)
[310 FS	58 FW]	['LF']	[F-16C/D]	Luke (to AE&TC 01/07/93)
[311 FS	58 FW]	['LF']	[F-16C/D]	Luke (to AE&TC 01/07/93)
[312 FS	58 FW]	['LF']	[F-16C/D]	Luke < <DISBANDED > >
[314 FS	58 FW]	['LF']	[F-16C/D]	Luke (to AE&TC 01/07/93)
389 FS	366 OG 366 WG	'MO'	F-16C	Mountain Home
4 FS	388 OG 388 FW	'HL'	F-16C (ex F-16A)	Hill
[16 TFTS	388 TFW]	['HL']	[F-16A]	Hill < <DISBANDED ../06/86> >
34 FS	388 OG 388 FW	'HL'	F-16C (ex F-16A)	Hill
421 FS	388 OG 388 FW	'HL'	F-16C (ex F-16A)	Hill
[428 TFS	474 TFW]	['NA']	[F-16A]	Nellis < <DISBANDED ../09/89> >
[429 TFS	474 TFW]	['NA']	[F-16A]	Nellis < <DISBANDED ../09/89> >
[430 TFS	474 TFW]	['NA']	[F-16A]	Nellis < <DISBANDED ../09/89> >

UNITED STATES AIR FORCES EUROPE

3rd Air Force

[527 AS	81 TFW]	['WR']	[F-16C]	Bentwaters < <DISBANDED ../10/90> >

16th Air Force

510 FS	31 OG 31 FW	'AV'	F-16C	Aviano
[512 FS	31 OG 31 FW]	['AV']	[F-16C]	Aviano (redesignated 510 FS)
555 FS	31 OG 31 FW	'AV'	F-16C	Aviano
[612 FS	401 FW]	['TJ']	[F-16C] (ex F-16A)	Torrejon < <DISBANDED ../10/91> >
[613 FS	401 FW]	['TJ']	[F-16C] (ex F-16A)	Torrejon < <DISBANDED 28/06/91> >
[614 FS	401 FW]	['TJ']	[F-16C] (ex F-16A)	Torrejon < <DISBANDED 30/12/91> >

17th Air Force

[10 FS	50 FW]	['HR']	[F-16C] (ex F-16A)	Hahn < <DISBANDED 30/09/91> >
[313 FS	50 FW]	['HR']	[F-16C] (ex F-16A)	Hahn < <DISBANDED 30/09/91> >
[496 FS	50 FW]	['HR']	[F-16C] (ex F-16A)	Hahn < <DISBANDED 30/09/91> >
22 FS	52 OG 52 FW	'SP'	F-16C	Spangdahlem (ex 480 FS)
23 FS	52 OG 52 FW	'SP'	F-16C	Spangdahlem
[81 FS	52 OG 52 FW]	['SP']	[F-16C]	Spangdahlem < <DISBANDED 1994> >
[480 FS	52 OG 52 FW]	['SP']	[F-16C]	Spangdahlem (to 22 FS)
[512 FS	86 OG 86 WG]	['RS']	[F-16C]	Ramstein (to 31 FW)
[526 FS	86 OG 86 WG]	['RS']	[F-16C]	Ramstein < <DISBANDED 01/07/94> >

(To Aviano as 31 FW 31/03/94)

UNITED STATES AIR FORCE – PACIFIC AIR FORCES

5th Air Force

13 FS	35 OG 35 FW	'MJ'	F-16C	Misawa
14 FS	35 OG 35 FW	'MJ'	F-16C	Misawa
[13 FS	432 OG 432 FW]	['MJ']	[F-16C] (ex F-16A)	Misawa (redesignated 35 FW 1995)
[14 FS	432 OG 432 FW]	['MJ']	[F-16C] (ex F-16A)	Misawa (redesignated 35 FW 1995)

7th Air Force

Squadron	Wing	Code	Type	Base
35 FS	8 OG 8 FW	'WP'	F-16C (ex F-16A)	Kunsan
80 FS	8 OG 8 FW	'WP'	F-16C (ex F-16A)	Kunsan
36 FS	51 OG 51 WG	'OS'	F-16C	Osan

11th Air Force

[18 FS	343 OG 343 WG]	['AK']	[F-16C]	Eielson (redesignated 354 WG 1994)
18 FS	354 OG 354 WG	'AK'	F-16C	Eielson

UNITED STATES AIR FORCE – AIR NATIONAL GUARD

107 FS	127 FW	'MI'	F-16C (ex F-16A)	Selfridge, Michigan ANG
111 FS	147 FG	—	F-16A (ADF)	Ellington, Texas ANG
112 FS	180 FG	'OH'	F-16C	Toledo, Ohio ANG
113 FS	181 FG	'TH'	F-16C	Terre Haute, Indiana ANG (ex 'HF')
114 FS	142 FG	—	F-16A (ADF)	Kingsley Field, Oregon ANG
119 FS	177 FG	—	F-16C (ex F-16A (ADF))	Atlantic City, New Jersey ANG
120 FS	140 FW	'CO'	F-16C	Buckley, Colorado ANG
121 FS	113 FW	'DC'	F-16C (ex F-16A)	Andrews, District of Columbia ANG
124 FS	132 FW	'IA'	F-16C	Des Moines, Iowa ANG
125 FS	138 FG	'OK'	F-16C	Tulsa, Oklahoma ANG
[127 FS	184 FG]	—	[F-16C]	McConnell, Kansas ANG (to B-1B)
134 FS	158 FG	—	F-16C (ex F-16A (ADF))	Burlington, Vermont ANG
[136 FS	107 FG]	—	[F-16A (ADF)]	Niagara Falls, New York ANG (to KC-135R)
138 FS	174 FW	'NY'	F-16C (ex F-16A)	Syracuse, New York ANG
148 FS	162 FG	—	F-16A/B	Tucson, Arizona ANG
149 FS	192 FG	'VA'	F-16C	Richmond, Virginia ANG
152 FS	162 FG	'AZ'	F-16C/D (ex F-16A/B)	Tucson, Arizona ANG
157 FS	169 FG	['SC']	F-16A	McEntire, South Carolina ANG
159 FS	125 FG	'FL'	F-16A (ADF)	Jacksonville, Florida ANG
160 FS	187 FG	'AL'	F-16C (ex F-16A)	Montgomery, Alabama ANG
[161 FS	184 FG]	—	[F-16C/D]	McConnell, Kansas ANG < <DISBANDED 01/08/94 > >
162 FS	178 FG	'OH'	F-16C	Springfield, Ohio ANG
163 FS	122 FW	'FW'	F-16C	Fort Wayne, Indiana ANG
[169 FS	182 FG]	['IL']	[F-16 A (ADF)]	Peoria, Illinois ANG (to C-130E)
170 FS	183 FG	'SI'	F-16C (ex F-16A)	Springfield, Illinois ANG
[171 FS	191 FG]	—	[F-16A (ADF)]	Selfridge, Michigan ANG (to C-130E)
174 FS	185 FG	—	F-16C	Sioux City, Iowa ANG
175 FS	114 FG	'SD'	F-16C	Sioux Falls, South Dakota ANG
176 FS	128 FW	'WI'	F-16C	Traux, Wisconsin ANG
[177 FS	184 FG]	—	[F-16C/D] (ex F-16A/B)	McConnell, Kansas ANG < <DISBANDED 01/08/94 > >
178 FS	119 FG	—	F-16A (ADF)	Fargo, North Dakota ANG
179 FS	148 FG	—	F-16A (ADF)	Duluth, Minnesota ANG
182 FS	149 FG	'SA'	F-16A	Kelly, Texas ANG
184 FS	188 FG	'FS'	F-16A	Fort Smith, Arkansas ANG
186 FS	120 FG	—	F-16A (ADF)	Great Falls, Montana ANG
188 FS	150 FG	'NM'	F-16C	Kirtland, New Mexico ANG
194 FS	144 FW	—	F-16C (ex F-16A (ADF))	Fresno, California ANG

Squadron	Wing	Code	Type	Base
195 FS	162 FG	'AZ'	F-16C (ex F-16A)	Tucson, Arizona ANG
198 FS	156 FG	'PR'	F-16A (ADF)	San Juan, Puerto Rico ANG

The 114, 178, 179, 184 & 186 FS to convert to F-16C in 1996

UNITED STATES AIR FORCE – AIR FORCE RESERVE

10th Air Force

Squadron	Wing	Code	Type	Base
[89 FS	906 FG 482 FW]	['DO']	[F-16A]	Wright-Patterson (to C-141B)
93 FS	915 FG 482 FW	'FM'	F-16A	Homestead
302 FS	944 FG 419 FW	'LR'	F-16C	Luke
457 FS	301 OG 301 FW	'TF'	F-16C	Carswell
465 FS	507 FG 301 FW	'SH'	F-16A	Tinker
466 FS	419 OG 419 FW	'HI'	F-16C (ex F-16A)	Hill
704 FS	924 FG 301 FW	'TX'	F-16C (ex F-16A)	Bergstrom
706 FS	926 FG 434 WG	'NO'	F-16C	New Orleans

UNITED STATES NAVY

[NFWS]	'Topgun'	—	[T/F-16N]	Miramar (F-16 disposed of 1995)
[VF-43]	'Challengers'	['AD']	[T/F-16N]	Oceana < <DISBANDED ../07/94> >
VF-45	'Blackbirds'	'AD'	T/F-16N	Key West
[VF-126]	'Bandits'	['NJ']	[F-16N]	Miramar < <DISBANDED ../09/94> >

BAHRAIN AMIRI AIR FORCE

			Type	Base
?			F-16C/D	Sheik Isa

BELGIAN AIR FORCE

Squadron	Wing	Type	Base
OCS	1 Wing	F16A/B	Beauvechain
1 Sqn	2 Wing	F-16A	Florennes
2 Sqn	2 Wing	F-16A	Florennes
23 Sqn	10 Wing	F-16A	Kleine-Brogel
31 Sqn	10 Wing	F-16A	Kleine-Brogel
349 Sqn	1 Wing	F-16A	Beauvechain
350 Sqn	1 Wing	F-16A	Beauvechain

No.1 Wing due to disband 03/96, with OCS and 349 Sqn. to transfer to 10 Wing and 350 Sqn. to 2 Wing.

ROYAL DANISH AIR FORCE

Squadron		Type	Base
Esk 723		F-16A	Aalborg
Esk 726		F-16A	Aalborg
Esk 727		F-16A	Skrydstrup
Esk 730		F-16A	Skrydstrup

EGYPTIAN AIR FORCE

Squadron	Wing	Type	Base
73 TFS	232 TFB	F-16A	Inchas
74 TFS	232 TFB	F-16A	Inchas
? TFS	242 TFB	F-16C	Beni Sueif
? TFS	242 TFB	F-16C	Beni Sueif
? TFS	? TFB	F-16C	Abu Sueir ?
? TFS	? TFB	F-16C	Saqqara

GREEK AIR FORCE

Squadron	Wing	Type	Base
330 Moira	111 Pterix	F-16C	Nea Anghialos
346 Moira	111 Pterix	F-16C	Nea Anghialos

INDONESIAN AIR FORCE

Squadron	Wing	Type	Base
3 Skw.	300 Wing	F-16A	Ishwahyudi AB, Madiun

ISRAELI AIR FORCE

Squadron	Wing	Code	Type	Base
101 Sqn			F-16C/D	Hatzor
105 Sqn			F-16C/D	Hatzor
109 Sqn			F-16C/D	Ramat David
110 Sqn			F-16C/D	Ramat David
117 Sqn			F-16C/D (ex F-16A)	Ramat David
140 Sqn			F-16A/B	Ramon
144 Sqn			F-16A/B	Hatzor
147 Sqn			F-16A/B	Ramon
190 Sqn			F-16A/B	Ramon
253 Sqn			F-16A/B	Ramon

ROYAL NETHERLANDS AIR FORCE

Squadron	Wing	Code	Type	Base
[TCA]			[F-16A/B]	Leeuwarden < <DISBANDED> >
306 Sqn			F-16A	Volkel
311 Sqn			F-16A	Volkel
312 Sqn			F-16A	Volkel
313 Sqn			F-16A	Twenthe
314 Sqn			F-16A	Gilze-Rijen (to disband 01/01/96)
315 Sqn			F-16A	Twenthe
[316 Sqn]			[F-16A]	Eindhoven < <DISBANDED 01/04/94> >
322 Sqn			F-16A	Leeuwarden
323 Sqn			F-16A	Leeuwarden

ROYAL NORWEGIAN AIR FORCE

Squadron	Wing	Code	Type	Base
331 Skv			F-16A	Bodo
332 Skv			F-16A	Rygge
334 Skv			F-16A	Bodo
338 Skv			F-16A	Oerland

PAKISTAN AIR FORCE

Squadron	Wing	Code	Type	Base
Combat Command School			F-16A/B	Sargodha
9 Sqn 'Griffins'			F-16A	Sargodha
11 Sqn 'Arrows'			F-16A/B	Sargodha
14 Sqn 'Shaheens'			F-16A	Kamra

PORTUGUESE AIR FORCE

Squadron	Wing	Code	Type	Base
201 Esc			F-16A/B	Monte Real

REPUBLIC OF (SOUTH) KOREA AIR FORCE

Squadron	Wing	Code	Type	Base
161 TFS	11 TFW		F-16C	Taegu
162 TFS	11 TFW		F-16C	Taegu

SINGAPORE DEFENCE FORCE

Squadron	Wing	Code	Type	Base
140 Sqn			F-16A/B	Tengah

ROYAL THAI AIR FORCE

Squadron	Wing	Code	Type	Base
103 Sqn	1 Wing		F-16A	Korat, Nakhon Ratchasima
403 Sqn	4 Wing		F-16A	Takhli

TURKISH AIR FORCE

Squadron	Wing	Code	Type	Base
Oncel Filo	4 Wing		F-16C/D	Murted
141 Filo	4 Wing		F-16C	Murted
142 Filo	4 Wing		F-16C	Murted
161 Filo	6 Wing		F-16C	Bandirma
162 Filo	6 Wing		F-16C	Bandirma
191 Filo	9 Wing		F-16C	Balikesir
192 Filo	9 Wing		F-16C	Balikesir

VENEZUELAN AIR FORCE

Squadron	Wing	Code	Type	Base
161 'Caribes' Esc		16 Grupo	F-16A	El Libertador
162 'Gavilanes' Esc		16 Grupo	F-16A	El Libertador